SLIGO
Sinbad's Yellow Shore

For Frank and Mary
with every good wish
and my blessing.

+ Thomas Finnegan-
Octbr 1992

SLIGO

Sinbad's Yellow Shore

by

T. A. FINNEGAN

When I look at my brother's picture, 'Memory Harbour' — houses and anchored ship and distant lighthouse all set close together as in some old map — I recognize in the blue-coated man with the mass of white shirt the pilot I went fishing with, and I am full of disquiet and of excitement, and I am melancholy because I have not made more and better verses. I have walked on Sinbad's yellow shore and never shall another's hit my fancy.

W. B. YEATS : *Autobiographies*

KEOHANES

Sligo – Ballina

Published by

KEOHANES
Sligo – Ballina

First published 1977
Reprinted 1978
Revised edition 1989

ISBN 0 85105 332 7 KEOHANES

Contents

Contents

Introduction

Everyone has heard of W. B. Yeats's Lake Isle of Innisfree. This book was written on another island well known
to the poet — Coney Island near Rosses Point. Few know
that this is Dorren's Island which features in his *Mythologies*. It is also 'our own, and the earlier, Coney Island'
mentioned in Jack B. Yeats's book, *Sligo*.

Coney Island lies in the mouth of Sligo Bay, a stone's
throw from the ruins of Elsinore Lodge in Rosses Point
where the Yeats brothers spent their long summer holidays as boys. It was in this region, guarded by Ben Bulben
on the north and Knocknarea on the south, that Sligo
became their Paradise.

> The wind is old and still at play
> While I must hurry upon my way,
> For I am running to Paradise.

The shadow of Knocknarea falls on Coney Island. For
that reason the warning of Seán O'Faoláin should be
sounded: 'Objectivity is impossible where so many reli-
ques excite the mind; dolmens, cairns, stone circles, forts,
cromlechs, trilithons, all suggestive of events not merely
great but superhuman. One look at that flat-topped
plateau of Knocknarea, one hint of its associations, one
glimpse of the enormous cairn surmounting it — as large
at close quarters as one of those man-dwarfing slag-heaps
of the Black Country — is enough to subdue all disbelief.'
(*An Irish Journey*).

Readers who have not yet come under the spell of
Knocknarea will be looking for chapter and verse for
everything. In an effort to satisfy these I have added some
notes, very reluctantly, because notes are a distraction —
they interfere with the flow of the narrative. I strongly
urge readers to ignore the notes until they come upon

them at the end. To reward those who do so, I have tried to make the notes interesting reading in themselves by including in them additional information, and by expanding the more important comments and explanations.

T.A.F.

1 Sligo

Sligo at last; beautiful descent into; beautiful town and region altogether. — Carlyle[1]

When he visited Ireland in 1849 Thomas Carlyle had scarcely a good word for any other part of the country. Even Killarney he damns with faint praise: 'rather beautiful, by contrast especially; well enough, but don't bother me with audibly admiring it.' As he entered Sligo by the road now known as Pearse Road, he was entranced by the scene before him.

Some years earlier, another perceptive traveller wrote:

The situation of Sligo is beautiful: it stands in a richly cultivated and finely wooded country. A magnificent bay, with lofty banks, lies to the west: a fine river flows through the town; and towards the east, the banks of the river upwards are redolent of every kind of beauty, and soon expand into Lock Gilly — one of the most lovely of the Irish lakes. — Inglis[2]

Situated on a wooded plain between Lough Gill and the sea, Sligo town derives its name from *Sligeach*, meaning 'the Shelly River', which was the ancient name for the River Garavogue on which it is built.

Lough Gill, the setting for Patrick G. Smith's stirring novel, *The Wild Rose of Lough Gill*, is one of the loveliest and most romantic of Irish lakes. Its many islands include Church Island (so called from its medieval church destroyed by fire in 1416), the seat of the O Cuirnín family, hereditary poets and historiographers of the O'Rourkes of Breifne,[3] and the small Isle of Innisfree which has been immortalised by the poet W. B. Yeats in his lyric 'The Lake Isle of Innisfree'.[4] Within two miles of the town, a panoramic view of Lough Gill is possible from 'the green road' on Cairns Hill or from wooded Dooney Rock which inspired Yeats's poem 'The Fiddler of Dooney'.[5]

As a town, Sligo is first mentioned in history when it was plundered and burned by the Vikings in 807; but its importance as a town dates from the middle of the thirteenth century when Maurice Fitzgerald came to live here, having first built his castle near the east end of the present Castle Street.

A century ago, an average of 500 ships visited Sligo port every year. Sligo ships traded with Canadian, Mediterranean and Black Sea ports. The largest Sligo ship owners were the Middletons and the Pollexfens. During the first half of the last century they owned a large fleet of sailing vessels. In 1856 they decided to use steam and by 1865 their steamships, *Sligo* and *Liverpool*, were regular callers at cross-channel ports. In 1865 they formed a company called 'The Sligo Steam Navigation Company' which owned a number of vessels in the Black Sea and Mediterranean grain trade.[6] Towards the end of the century their involvement in shipping declined. In 1880 they had four small ships. By 1890 the only ship owned by the company was the schooner *Sea*. By the end of the century she too had gone and the company gave up ship-owning.[7]

Sligo and its surroundings were a life-long inspiration to the poet and playwright, W. B. Yeats. Yeats's father and mother came from Sligo and, though they moved to London when he was a year old, the poet spent his boyhood holidays in Sligo. Most of his summers were spent in Rosses Point, at Elsinore Lodge which still stands, sadly deserted and decaying, beside the newly reconstructed pier.[8] 'The place that really influenced my life was Sligo,' declared the Nobel Prize winning poet.[9]

The poet's brother, Jack B. Yeats, the celebrated artist, wrote (towards the end of his life): 'I never did a painting without putting a thought of Sligo in it.' An early painting of Jack Yeats, entitled 'Memory Harbour', captures an impression of Rosses Point when the artist and his brother spent their long summer holidays there a century ago. There are ships in the picture, and seafaring men, thatched cottages and whitewashed taverns; Coney Island is in it, and the Metal Man standing guard over the entrance to Sligo port.[10] 'Sligo is indeed the rock out of which the two great brothers have been hewn.' [11]

Sligo is unique. It is the only county along this seaboard which has been civilised. Who civilised it is not for me to say. It spills over the border of Donegal into Ballyshannon and over the borders of Roscommon into Boyle. And, for a cyclist, it is extraordinary, having cycled for days through the wilds of Donegal and Mayo, to emerge at Bundoran or Ballysodare into this gracious country with its lovely landscapes and poetic feeling. I shall never forget arriving one evening, wet and exhausted, at Bundoran and going into the lounge of the hotel, where a little orchestra from Sligo was playing a selection of Carolan's airs. That is certainly something you would not hear anywhere else in Ireland.   — Frank O'Connor[12]

2   Coney Island

Coney Island off Co. Sligo is remarkably isolated. The approach is by water, except at low tide when a kind of causeway, perhaps the remains of something more ambitious, emerges. . . . Coney, like many of the islands off the west coast of Ireland, is gradually being abandoned by the inhabitants, many of the cottages stand empty, there is even a house of several stories, still filled with furniture, which has been left to decay. Except for a few conifers round this house, Coney has almost no trees, the arch of the sky seems enormous, and the stretch of the ocean immense. Sailing west from Coney the next land is America, three thousand miles away.
— Cecil Woodham-Smith[1]

Mrs. Woodham-Smith, author of *The Great Hunger*, spent a holiday on Coney Island. Among many other people who did likewise was Owen Tweedy, the traveller and writer, who often stayed for three months at a time. He wrote:

I have the same sort of feeling here that I've had when looking at the pyramids — of something which has seen a lot and knows a lot. Perhaps it's because this is an island and a very small one. Perhaps it's because it's so perfect a setting. It is a delectable island.[2]

There is a tradition that Coney Island, New York, got its name from Sligo's Coney Island. This is possible and, indeed, likely. Sligo itself has given its name to three towns in North America.[3] The story of the naming of the American Coney Island is well known.

In the last century, the merchant ship *Arethusa* used to sail between Sligo and North America. In those days the American Coney Island, lying just offshore and swarming with rabbits, was unnamed. The captain of the *Arethusa*, which was owned by Sligo man, Peter O'Connor, named it after his own very similar Coney Island in Sligo Bay.[4]

The name Coney Island means, in Irish, 'the island of rabbits'. To those who know the Irish Coney Island well this is an obvious name. Its sand dunes have always housed large colonies of rabbits. Repeated outbreaks of disease have failed to wipe out the hardy island strain. The dunes in which most of the rabbits reside are on the south side of the island (opposite Knocknarea) and, unlike the blown sand dunes on the north side, suffer little from sea or wind erosion. They are speckled with a great variety of wild flowers including kidney-vetch, thyme and various orchids.[5]

Though Inishmulclohy (Mulclohy's Island) is the more ancient name of the island,[6] it was well known as Coney Island in the days of the Cromwellian Plantation. For the benefit of readers unfamiliar with the story of Cromwell in Ireland, the following extract from John C. McTernan's *Historic Sligo* will be of interest (the author is dealing with 'successive attempts of the British Government to confiscate Irish lands and plant them with British settlers and adventurers').

The Cromwellian Settlement of mid-17th century was the most ambitious of such undertakings. It consisted of wholesale allotments of Irish lands to officers of the Parliamentary troops in lieu of wages. About 1653, large tracts of the best land in Co. Sligo, amounting to

63,000 acres, were divided amongst the disbanded Cromwellian officers and soldiers. The quantity of land given to each was in proportion to the amount of pay due. The Cromwellian Settlement was an effective method of colonisation. Within a few years the old Sligo families, the O'Connors, O'Harts, O'Dowds, O'Garas, Mc-Donaghs and some of the O'Haras were dispossessed. Their places were taken by the settlers, the Coopers, Woods, Percevals, Wynnes, Irwins, Ormsbys, Croftons and Gores whose descendants have figured prominently in the affairs of the county.[7]

Cromwell's original idea was 'to hell or to Connacht', that is, to leave all the province of Connacht (and Co. Clare) for the native Irish who survived the campaign. However, when the adventurers and high-ranking officers had received their allocations in Ulster, Leinster and Munster, insufficient land was available for the rest of the soldiers. Their allocation was made up in Connacht from the lands of Sligo, Leitrim and part of Mayo.[8]

In Cromwell's proposals for planting the Sligo region, the 'lands on the mile-line, together with two little islands called Oyster Island and Coney Island (containing 200 acres), were leased for one year from 10th April, 1655 for the use of such English families as should come from New England and America'.[9]

It is uncertain whether any English families ever came to the islands at the time. According to the historian Terence O'Rorke none came.[10] It is certain, however, that in the seventeenth century Coney Island was an attractive piece of land commercially. In Boate's *Natural History of Ireland*, published in 1653 for the benefit of the Cromwellian planters, the author states that in his day there were in all of Ireland only three silver and lead mines; one of these was 'in Connaught, upon the very harbour mouth of Sligo, in a little desert island called Coney Island.'[11]

Coney Island, 'rich in legend and folk-lore dating back to the time of St. Patrick,'[12] is five minues by boat from Rosses Point. It can be reached overland, at low tide, from a point near Strandhill on the opposite side of the harbour.[13]

For the ageing traveller, Owen Tweedy, who spent many summers on Coney Island:

the best time of the day is when the sun goes down over the Atlantic and the island settles in for the night. The cries of the seagulls are stilled; the horses slowly plod home from the day's work; the cows have been milked and swing back placidly to their fields; and the hens and the ducks and the geese and the turkeys gossip quietly on their nightly way home. And in the stillness I can hear from my cottage the rush of the tide swirling through Shrulnamíle — the channel of a thousand streams; and from away in the west comes the deep rumble of the great Atlantic rollers as they crash their way up Carty's Strand.[14]

At the turn of this century there was a population of about one hundred on Coney Island. Parnell visited the island to address the inhabitants. In the 1950's, when Owen Tweedy was living and writing on the island, the population was twenty-six. Today the island's population is nine. They are: senior citizens, Michael James Ward, Mrs. Tessie McGowan, Miss Katie Haran and Tommy McLoughlin; John McGowan, his wife Margaret, and their three young children.[15]

Youthful octogenarian Michael James Ward, the island's publican, gives this advice to new visitors to Coney Island:

Take the green road along the shore by the two black beacons, and do the circle of the island. I guarantee you'll see more of Sligo than you ever saw before. You'll see the church towers in the east, and Ben Bulben to the north, and the Bay to the west; and the little sailing boats and the seagulls after the mackerel; you'll see Rosses Point and Dead Man's Point; you'll see as far as Drumcliff and Lissadell; you'll see "the man who never told a lie" — the Metal Man; you'll see the Wishing Chair and Killaspugbrón, but keep your wishing for another day because you can wish only once a year. You'll see Carty's White Strand and that cave on Carraig Mairtín; you'll see the old fort at the back of the island, and if you're lucky you'll see a fairy or two there. As you come round by the sand hills you'll see Knocknarea and Dunán Pádraig to the south; and as you finish the circle you'll have Cummen Strand and the fourteen Pillars on your right hand. What more could you ask for?

While walking along the green road, one should pause occasionally and turn from the vast beauty outside the island to the delicate beauty alongside the little road. I remember a sunny August evening when my mother and her friend Margaret O'Boyle returned from the Wishing Chair, one with a lovely bouquet of woodbine, the other with a hatful of shining blackberries.[16]

This is a low-lying, flat but verdant isle in a most beautiful setting, with fine views across Sligo Bay and to Knocknarea Mountain, only 1,078 feet high, but in this setting having all the appearance of a majestic peak.[17]

3   The Church Towers

One Summer night, when there was peace, a score of Puritan troopers, under the pious Sir Frederick Hamilton, broke through the door of the Abbey of the White Friars at Sligo. As the door fell with a crash they saw a little knot of friars gathered about the altar, their white habits glimmering in the steady light of the holy candles. All the monks were kneeling except the abbot who stood upon the altar steps with a great brass crucifix in his hand. "Shoot them", cried Sir Frederick Hamilton, but nobody stirred, for all were new converts, and feared the candles and the crucifix. For a little while all were silent and then five troopers, who were the bodyguard of Sir Frederick Hamilton, lifted their muskets, and shot down five of the friars. The noise and the smoke drove away the mystery of the pale altar lights, and the other troopers took courage and began to strike. In a moment the friars lay about the altar steps, their white habits stained with blood. "Set fire to the house", cried Sir Frederick Hamilton, and a trooper carried in a heap of dry straw, and piled it against the western wall, but did not light it, because he was still afraid of crucifix and of candles. Seeing this, the five troopers who were Sir Frederick Hamilton's bodyguard went up to the altar, and taking each a holy candle set the straw ablaze.

— W. B. Yeats[1]

15

The square tower on the arms of the Borough of Sligo is that of the Abbey of the White Friars or Dominicans.[2] The present arms are practically the same as those adopted in 1613 when Sligo was incorporated as a parliamentary borough. Twenty-nine years later, on the night of 1 July 1642, the soldiers of Sir Frederick Hamilton sacked the town of Sligo, killing every visible inhabitant. They 'fell upon the Abbey, set fire to everything they could, within and without the church and conventual buildings, and burned altars, altar ornaments, vestments, and various articles of value committed by the townspeople for safe keeping to the friars.'[3] It is believed that all the friars were killed. A legend persists that the silver bell of the ruined abbey lies at the bottom of Lough Gill; and only the perfect are privileged to hear it when on occasion it peals over the city.

The Abbey is 'Sligo's most distinguished architectural treasure'[4] and the only medieval building which survives in the city. Its elaborately carved stone high altar is the only one remaining in any Irish monastic ruin. The Abbey was founded in 1252 by Maurice Fitzgerald for the friars of the Dominican Order. Accidentally destroyed by fire (from a candle) in 1414, in the springtime of the year, it was almost immediately rebuilt in its present style. It is the burial place of kings and princes including Tighernan O'Rourke, King of Breifne, who died in 1418, and successive chiefs of the O'Connor Sligo clan.[5]

The tower of the Abbey cannot be seen from Coney Island, but that of the Cathedral of the Immaculate Conception can; and on a calm day the striking clock and the pealing bells can be heard across the Bay. The time can be read on the Cathedral tower with the aid of a telescope or good binoculars.

The Cathedral was built by Bishop Laurence Gillooly to the design of George Goldie of London, one of the three chief architects of the last century. It was consecrated on 26 July 1874 and completed in the following year. In 1975 its centenary was marked by a renovation undertaken by the present Bishop of Elphin, Most Reverend Dominic Conway.[6]

Beside the Cathedral stands the Church of St. John the Baptist (Church of Ireland) which was designed in 1730 by the famous German architect, Cassels, who also designed Hazelwood House, Sligo, Leinster House, Dublin (the seat of the Irish Government), Powerscourt, Co. Wicklow, and Carton House, Co. Kildare.[7]

The religion in general Catholic : but more Protestants than in any other county in Connaught.

— Arthur Young on County Sligo in 1776[8]

4 Ben Bulben

Under bare Ben Bulben's head
In Drumcliff churchyard Yeats is laid.
An ancestor was rector there
Long years ago, a church stands near,
By the road an ancient cross.
No marble, no conventional phrase;
On limestone quarried near the spot
By his command these words are cut :
    Cast a cold eye
    On life, on death.
    Horseman, pass by !

— W. B. Yeats

The poem 'Under Ben Bulben' has been called Yeats's last will and testament. It is a poem of six stanzas which he commenced in August 1938 and was still correcting only two days before he died on 28 January 1939.[1]

Flat-topped Ben Bulben, a carboniferous limestone plateau, stands to the north of Sligo and Coney Island. The name in Irish means 'Gulban's Peak', called after Conall Gulban, a son of Niall of the Nine Hostages, who was fostered there. Niall was a fifth-century prince of

17

Connacht who became High King of Ireland and won fame and power by successful raids on Britain. From his brothers, Brión and Fiachra, descended the great ruling families of Connacht. Three of his sons, including Conall, founded kingdoms in Ulster and their descendants adopted the now famous dynastic name, Uí Néill. St. Columba (Colmcille) was a great-grandson of Conall Gulban.

Though nearly two thousand feet high, Ben Bulben is capped by a peat-like soil with dense vegetation containing plants which have attracted the attention of botanists from home and abroad.[2] In the last century dozens of alpine plant species were counted on Ben Bulben. More recent expeditions have added many more to the list, including several maritime species. The abundance and variety of alpine and arctic-alpine plants on Ben Bulben has made it an ecological and botanical area of international rating. A few of its species are not found elsewhere in these islands, and several others have not been recorded elsewhere in Ireland.[3]

A section of the Ben Bulben range contains rich deposits of barytes, a mineral which is in demand at present in rotary drilling for petroleum.[4]

Ben Bulben has long figured in Irish legend and history. It is the scene of the final episode of the best known of our epic love tales, 'The Pursuit of Diarmaid and Gráinne'.[5] Because of the importance of this epic in Irish literature, a summary of its story is given in the following chapter.[6]

5 The Pursuit of Diarmaid and Gráinne

Diarmaid O Duibhne was a member of the Fianna, the renowned standing army of the High King of Ireland, Cormac Mac Airt, who began his reign in 254 A.D. Diarmaid was a noble-minded, generous young man, of untarnished honour, and the bravest of the brave. Handsome as he was valiant, he was known as 'Diarmaid of the Bright Face' and 'Diarmaid of the White Teeth'. He was also endowed with a 'love-spot', a birth mark or mole (called *ball seirce* in Irish), which made him 'the favourite of maidens'.

Gráinne was the High King's daughter. Of all the maidens of Ireland she was the most beautiful, the best instructed and the most discreet in speech and manner.

The commander-in-chief of the Fianna was Fionn Mac Cumhaill who was a man of supreme military ability, brave and wise but also unforgiving to those who injured him. He was possessed of two preternatural gifts received after he tasted the Salmon of Knowledge (caught in the River Boyne). These were: the gift of foreknowledge; and the power of healing from sickness or wounds, even though the person should be at the point of death, by giving a drink of water from the closed palms of his hands.[1]

Fionn's wife died, and he wished to marry again. His closest advisors were his son, Oisín, and Diorraing, both members of the Fianna. These considered the King's daughter, Gráinne, worthy in all respects to be the wife of Fionn. Because of an old disagreement between Fionn and the King, Fionn asked Oisín and Diorraing to go to Tara in his name and ask the maiden for him. 'If the King should refuse,' he said, 'so let it be; but I can more easily bear a refusal given to you than to myself.'

19

Gráinne made this reply to her father: 'I do not know whether Fionn is worthy to be your son-in-law; but if he is, why should he not be a fitting husband for me?'

The marriage was arranged, though Fionn was older than Gráinne's father. The King arranged a great feast at which Fionn was to claim his young bride. During the festivities Gráinne rose from her seat and, walking softly across the hall, sat down near Diarmaid. With downcast eyes and low voice she said: 'Will you, Diarmaid, return my love if I give it to you?'

Diarmaid heard the princess with amazement and alarm. But, even before he was aware, his heart leaped with joy. When he remembered his duty to his chief, however, he hardened his mind and answered with cold looks and words: 'I will not love the maiden who is bethrothed to Fionn; and even if I were so minded, I dare not.'

With eyes still cast down, Gráinne said: 'I know well it is your duty, and not your heart, that prompts you to speak so. You see why I am forced to speak more boldly than a maiden should. Fionn has come to ask me for his wife, but he is an old man, even older than my father, and I do not love him. But I love you, Diarmaid, and I beseech you to save me from this hateful marriage.'

Diarmaid was sorely troubled. He strove within himself, but strove in vain; for he could not help loving the princess with his whole heart. Yet nonetheless did he hide his thoughts, for his duty to his chief prevailed. He spoke to his comrades and asked counsel of them. Oisín, son of Fionn, said: 'You are blameless, and I counsel you to love and follow Gráinne; but guard yourself against the wiles of Fionn.' And so counselled his other comrades of the Fiana, Oscar and Caoilte and Diorraing.

Then at last Diarmaid yielded and strove no longer; and putting off his sterness of manner and voice, he spoke gently to the princess: 'I will hide my thoughts from you

20

no more, Gráinne. I will be your husband, all unworthy of you as I am. I will guard you and defend you to the death from Fionn and his hirelings.'

For seven years Diarmaid and Gráinne avoided capture by the pursuing Fionn and his men. Their pursuit throughout the length and breadth of Ireland is one of the world's great tales of love and adventure.[2]

In the closing episode we discover Diarmaid, accompanied by his faithful hound, Mac-an-Choill, chasing a wild boar on the slopes of Ben Bulben. Against the advice of Gráinne he had been lured into the chase by the wily Fionn who was hunting the same boar with the Fianna. Gráinne had advised him to bring his great spear and great sword, but Diarmaid, regarding the matter lightly, answered: 'How can danger arise from such a small affair? I will bring the Beagaltach and the Ga Buidhe; and I will also bring Mac-an-Choill, leading him by his chain.'[3]

On the face of the hill Fionn and the Fianna discover the boar dead and Diarmaid 'lying pale and bleeding in the pangs of death.' And Fionn said: 'I am pleased, Diarmaid, to see you in this plight; but I am grieved that all the women of Ireland cannot see you also.'

Diarmaid asks Fionn to give him a drink of water from the closed palms of his hands. Fionn hesitates: 'You of all men least deserves it of me.' Diarmaid reminds Fionn of his past services to his chief. At this point Oscar, son of Oisín and grandson of Fionn, one of the most valiant and kind-hearted of the Fianna, intervenes. Moved with pity, even to tears, he addresses Fionn: 'Although I am nearer akin to you, my Chief, than to Diarmaid, I cannot suffer that he die, when a drink from your hands would heal him. Bring him a drink without delay.'

Fionn answered: 'I know of no well on this mountain from which to bring a drink.'

'Therein you speak not truth,' said Diarmaid, 'you

know that not more than nine paces from here, hidden under yonder bush, is a well of crystal water.'

Thereupon Fionn went to the well and, holding his two hands tightly together, he brought up some of the water, and came towards Diarmaid; but after he had walked a little way, he let it spill through his fingers, saying that he was not able to bring water in his hands so far.

'Not so, Fionn,' said Diarmaid, 'I saw that you of your own will did spill it. And now, Fionn, hasten, for death is on me.'

Again he went to the well, and was bringing the water slowly while Diarmaid followed the dripping hands with his eyes; but, when Fionn thought of Gráinne, he let the water spill a second time.

By this time Oscar was no longer able to contain his grief and rage. 'I swear, O Chief,' he said, 'if you do not bring the water, only one of us two — you or I — shall leave this hill alive.' Hearing Oscar's words, and seeing the frowning looks of the others, Fionn dipped up the water a third time and was hastening forward; but before he had got half-way, Diarmaid's head dropped backwards.

And all the Fianna present raised three long, loud cries of sorrow for Diarmaid O Duibhne.

Gráinne sat that day on the highest rampart of Rath-Gráinne, watching for Diarmaid's return; for a dark fear haunted her on account of this chase.' When at last the Fianna came in view, and she saw Diarmaid's dog led by Fionn, she fell forward off the rampart and lay in a swoon, while her handmaid and children stood over her, weeping and distracted.

When she opened her eyes, they told her that Diarmaid had perished by the wild boar of Ben Bulben. She and her women and all the people of her court raised three loud, bitter cries of lamentation, which were heard in the glens and wildernesses around, and which pierced the clouds of heaven.

When at last Gráinne became calm, she ordered that five hundred of her people should go to Ben Bulben to bring home the body of Diarmaid. Then, turning to Fionn, who still held Mac-an-Choill in his hand, she asked him to leave her Diarmaid's hound. But Fionn refused, saying that a hound was a small matter. When Oisín heard this, he came forward and took the hound from the hand of Fionn and gave him to Gráinne.

6 The Bay to the West

Spring in the air of it, a bright, keen day, and the mist only strong enough to soften the bold, rugged outline of Knocknarea, our sailing mark, towering high and solitary over Sligo Harbour. The strong west wind that we had fought and bested at the Stags turned friendly, had blown us fair to our voyage's end, and now, under easy canvas, we tacked on shore and off, waiting for tide to bear up and float our twenty feet in safety across the Bar.

The Brassbounder[1]

The Brassbounder, first published in 1910, is a classic of the sea from 'the days of sail'. It contains a vivid account of apprenticeship aboard a nineteenth-century windjammer, written by the apprentice himself, Glasgow-born David Bone who became a distinguished Captain of the British Merchant Navy and was knighted at the end of the Second World War. The sailing ship in the story was the *City of Florence* which took young David Bone on a long, arduous and sometimes perilous voyage round Cape Horn to San Francisco and back. At Falmouth, on the return journey, the Captain receives orders to proceed to Sligo.

"Sligo! Sligo, where's that anyway?"
"North of Ireland, sir," said M'Kellar. "Somewhere east of Broadhaven. I was in there once, myself."

"Of course; of course! Sligo, eh? Well, well! I never heard of a square-rigger discharging there — must see about th' charts. Ask them to repeat, Mister, and make sure".

The final chapter contains a graphic description of the barque's entry to Sligo Harbour, and the usual stop-over at Rosses Point before the long pull up to the town.

The land about is low to the coast, but far inland blue, mist-capped ranges stand bold and rugged against the clear northern sky. Beyond the Bar the harbour lies bare of shipping — only a few fishing skiffs putting out under long sweeps, and the channel buoys bobbing and heaving on the long swell. A deserted port we are come to after our long voyage from the West! . . .

A short tow, for all the bargaining, and at Rosses Point we bring up to moorings — the voyage at an end. . . .

The doors of the village inn swinging constantly, and the white-aproned landlord (mopping a heated brow at royal orders), sending messengers to ransack the village cupboards for a reserve of glasses. And then at last the boats are ready for the long pull up to Sligo town and the impatient boatmen shouting, "Coom on now, byes! Before th' toide tarns; byes, now!" The free men embark, and we, the afterguard (who draw no pay), are left to watch them set off, and wish that our day were quickly come.[2]

Michael James Ward had not heard of *The Brass-bounder* or the *City of Florence* — it was just another cargo vessel going up the channel to Sligo. But he had heard of the Norwegian timber ship, the *Narayana*, wrecked on the western rocks of Coney Island 'the night Luke Carty was born in 1890.' The crew survived. Michael James proudly points to the wall displaying a faded photograph of the bearded captain who was grateful for the prompt assistance and warm friendship of the islanders.

The wooden nameplate of one of the *Narayana* lifeboats is on display in Austie Gillen's at Rosses Point. One day Michael James pointed to an old house on the island. 'One of the cannons from the *Narayana* is buried behind that house,' he said. 'There was a time when we couldn't

24

keep guns on the island, not even cannons.' Shortly afterwards I took a few boys from my school to the island.
'Find the cannon,' I said. They did. It can now be seen
at John McGowan's on Coney Island.

From Michael James Ward I first heard the well-
known story of the Fenian ship *Erin's Hope* which lay at
anchor for six days off Coney Island. When the American
Civil War ended in 1865 considerable numbers of Irish-
American officers, trained in the Civil War, came to
Ireland to take part in the planned uprising of the Fenian
Movement which 'differed from all previous national
movements in that it drew its support not only from all
the Irish at home but also from the new Ireland that
emigration had created in Britain and the U.S.A. The
special function of the American body was to aid the
home organisation with arms and officers.'[3] The rising
intended for 1865 was postponed because the promised
arms did not arrive from the U.S.A.

After the attempted rising in March 1867, the 138-ton
brigantine, *Jackmel*, in the charge of American Fenian
officers, set sail from New York with a cargo of arms and
ammunition. The commander of the expedition was John
F. Kavanagh who had been a brigadier-general in the
American Civil War and was, at one time, a member of
the American Congress. The ship set sail without papers
or colours. To avoid suspicion the men embarked without
luggage and, for one day, sailed towards the West Indies.
Whenever vessels came in sight, English colours were
hoisted. In mid-Atlantic the officers changed the ship's
name to *Erin's Hope*. It arrived in Sligo Bay on 20 May
1867 but was refused permission to enter port. After
lying at anchor for six days it sailed back for New York.
At Helvick, thirty-one of the officers and men were put
ashore. Suspicious coastguards had them arrested. They
got heavy sentences, but none was executed.[4]

25

7 The Little Sailing Boats

New York is in my mind away out there a leap or two over high waves to the west. And down on the shores of our Bay, looking out through the horns of it, with the tall pale lighthouse on your southerly hand, the sun that is sinking wild and tattered here is glistening on the boys and girls of Coney Island — that is *their* Coney Island, not our own, and the earlier, Coney Island.   — Jack B. Yeats[1]

One evening on Coney Island, as the tide was turning and the sun going down, I walked with Michael James Ward across 'the Paddock' and slowly up the little hill at the back of his cottage. We sat down on the green rim of the old fort, gazing in silence at the golden bay which was dotted with the red and white sails of boats from Sligo Yacht Club. There was a fresh, westerly breeze.

After a long silence Michael James said, 'She won't get away.' We were both watching a small sailing dinghy which two boys were trying to steer away from the powerful currents between Coney Island and Oyster Island. The channel between the two islands is called Shrunamíle, Irish for 'the channel of a thousand currents.'

Michael James was right. The two young boys, the fresh breeze and the small white sails were no match for Shrunamíle. As the dinghy was swept past us, Michael James yelled, 'Go around Oyster.' The boys did not seem to hear him. An hour later, when the tide was full, we saw them paddling back to port with sails lowered.

Later that night, before a blazing timber fire, Michael James told me of the Regattas at Rosses Point and Raughley and Maugherow and Lough Gill. The Coney Islanders — the McGowans, the Cartys, the Harans and himself — brought home many prizes for sailing and rowing.[2]

According to the historian W. G. Wood-Martin, 'in 1821 yacht-racing seems first to have been regularly established in Sligo.'[3] On display in Sligo Museum is the sterling silver Ladies Cup presented as a perpetual challenge trophy by the ladies of Sligo to 'the racing community of Lough Gill.' It was first competed for in the year 1822. The handsome cup is a very fine example of Irish embossed work. Standing fourteen-and-a-half inches high and weighing sixty-eight ounces, it bears the mark of the Irish Goldsmiths for 1821. An inscription on it states that it was presented 'for the encouragement of fast sailing boats on Lough Gill.'

The 1876 Regatta on Lough Gill was marred by a very serious accident. A small yacht sank in one of the deepest parts of the lake, and her crew of four were drowned. Shortly afterwards, the same yacht, which had been raised from the lake, was almost swamped again at the Rosses Point Regatta.

About this time there was another serious mishap when one of the sturdy steamers of the Middleton-Pollexfen Line came to grief. Sheelah Kirby records the incident in *The Yeats Country* because one of the people on board was the father of Susan Pollexfen, mother of W. B. Yeats.

Towards Rosses Point the road follows the channel that runs from Sligo to the sea. Here the boy Yeats was shown one evening the lights of the outward-bound steamer with his grandfather on board. Next morning he heard the vessel was wrecked and eight men in it drowned.[4]

After the Lough Gill sailing accident in 1876 there was a revival of interest in rowing. A rowing club was established in 1879 and in the following year we find the Lough Gill Regatta being organised by 'Sligo Commercial Rowing Club' which put a special emphasis on races confined to 'professional oarsmen'.[5] Another accident, this time in a rowing race, occurred in the year 1881. One of the Club's own boats was swamped in a heavy breeze and two of the crew were drowned. Wood-Martin suggests that this accident may have been responsible for 'the decline of the amusement'.

On display in the fine new Rosses Point Pavilion of

Sligo Yacht Club are the printed programmes of Lough Gill Regattas held in the years 1903, 1905, 1906 and 1907. Lough Gill still provides winter quarters for the all-season enthusiasts of Sligo Yacht Club.

8   The Seagulls and the Mackerel

[Coney Islanders] know the sea like a book, and so for pollock we fish off the Perch Rock or the Black Rock or the Long Rock; and for mackerel we just watch the seagulls. And there are great evenings when the mackerel shoals are in; and then, with the gulls screaming and diving like mad all round us, we take so fast that our lines are scarcely in and out again before another fish is on.

— Owen Tweedy[1]

It is said that Coney Island suffered little from the Great Famine because, as Michael James Ward expressed it, 'the blight didn't harm the fish, thank God.' He was not referring to salmon, for which Sligo is famous, nor to oysters which were plentiful in those days. Such choice species were reserved for tables at which hunger was only a topic of conversation.

Michael James tells this story from his father's time. One snowy day his father and three more Coney Islanders were dredging for oysters in Drumcliff Bay. A group of mounted police appeared on the shore and fired shots at their boat. Michael's father agreed to go ashore to explain that he and his companions were rightfully fishing for oysters. When he stepped ashore he was promptly arrested and marched into Sligo. What annoyed Michael James most, as he told the story, was not the charge of illegal fishing brought against the Coney Islanders, but the thought of his father being forced to walk six or seven miles in snow while his captors were riding comfortably on horseback and his friends sailing leisurely back to the island.

Like the men of Aran and the men of the Donegal

28

Rosses, the men of Coney Island are never anxious to talk of those who were lost on the sea (I have never heard a Coney Islander use the word 'drowned'). It will suffice to say that the cruel sea has claimed lives in every generation. There are sore hearts still on Coney Island and in Rosses Point from the tragedy of 1950 when six men were lost, and the tragedy of 1972 when three men were lost, all in boating accidents.

9   Dead Man's Point

At a place, close to the Dead Man's Point, at the Rosses, where the disused pilot-house looks out to sea through two round windows like eyes, a mud cottage stood in the last century. It also was a watch-house, for a certain old Michael Bruen, who had been a smuggler, and was still the father and grandfather of smugglers, lived there, and when, after night-fall, a tall French schooner crept over the bay from Raughley, it was his business to hang a horn lantern in the southern window, that news might travel to Dorren's Island, and thence, by another horn lantern, to the village of the Rosses.
— W. B. Yeats[1]

The old pilot-house still stands on Dead Man's Point, a headland which juts out from Rosses Point village towards Coney Island. (Coney Island was sometimes called Dorren's Island after a family that once lived there.) Dead Man's Point is so called from a foreign seaman who, at the turn of the last century, died as his ship was entering port. He was, in the words of the poet Yeats (writing about his brother's painting 'Memory Harbour'), 'buried there by a ship's crew in a hurry not to miss the tide. As they were not sure if he was really dead, they buried him with a loaf, as the story runs. My brother painted the picture many years ago.'[2]

In the old days, Dead Man's Point, with its secluded landing spot in front of Elsinore Lodge, was a favourite haunt for smugglers. In the eighteenth century, according

29

to Wood-Martin, 'several people in a seemingly respectable sphere of life, lived principally by this secret traffic, which was then carried on in a business-like and wholesale manner.' [3] Tobacco apparently was the chief contraband. Coney Island has still a link with the days of tobacco smuggling. On the northern side, under the beacons which face the Strand at Rosses Point, is an area of shore called *Poll a' Tabac*, Irish for 'the tobacco hole'.

A public inquiry in Sligo in 1880 established the existence of oath-bound gangs of smugglers. 'Elsinore was built by a successful smuggler named John Black, who set several cannon outside it, as though to command the estuary.' [4] The Middletons believed that the house was haunted by smugglers. They often nervously listened for the three taps on the window pane. It is not surprising, therefore, that the young W. B. Yeats, who spent his summers at Elsinore, was filled with tales of fast cutters and daring smugglers. [5]

Dead Man's Point has long been noted for another reason. For nearly a century it has been an area of very interesting vegetation, most of which has survived the increased traffic of recent years. Those interested in botany will find here sea spleenworth, creeping willow, kidney-vetch and thyme; and—especially along the south side — blue moor grass, sheep's fescue, downy oat and spotted orchid. Parts of this area remind one of the Burren in Co. Clare. On Dead Man's Point you will find, if you search, burnet rose, crested hair grass and—without much searching — bluebell and a little heather.

10   Drumcliff

In the year 807, the dreaded Viking raiders made their first appearance off the coast of Sligo in their long, low ships. They plundered Innishmurray and, during subsequent raids, burned the town of Sligo and plundered the monastery at Drumcliff.[1]

Drumcliff (in Irish, 'the ridge of the hazels'[2]), lying in the shadow of Ben Bulben, was one of the most important places in Sligo in ancient times. According to *The Annals of the Four Masters*, St. Columba (521–597),also called Colmcille, founded a monastery there in the year 574. For many years it was a well-known seat of learning, frequented even by foreigners. The history of this monastery is recorded by the Four Masters up to the year 1503. All that remain of the foundation today are part of a Round Tower, the shaft of a plain cross and a thirteen-foot high sculptured cross of the tenth century which is regarded as a gem among Irish antiquities.[3] Among the exquisitely carved panels on the cross are sculptures of the Fall of Adam and Eve, and of the Crucifixion.

In the vicinity of Drumcliff is the ancient battlefield of Cooldruman (Cúl Dreimne in Irish) where in 553 (according to *The Annals of the Four Masters*; in 561 according to most other authorities) the famous Battle of the Books was fought over the first case of disputed copyright. St. Finian of Moville, with whom St. Columba had studied in former days, brought back from Rome a copy of the Psalms which he valued highly and which he did not wish Columba to copy. Columba, however, who was a dexterous and rapid scribe, secretly made a copy of the book; but Finian, learning this, claimed the copy.[4] Columba refused it, and the matter was referred to the High King, Diarmaid, at Tara. The nearest analogy which the King could find in ancient Irish law was 'to every cow her calf'. Accordingly, he decided in favour of Finian, saying, 'To every book its son-book, as to every cow her calf.'

Columba refused to accept Diarmaid's judgement. The king set forth from Tara with an army to recover the copy. He had been waiting for an opportunity to move against Columba in revenge for an unfortunate incident in which the King's friend, Curnán, was killed while under the protection of Columba. Columba, a Donegal man from Gartan, and a descendant of Niall of the Nine Hostages, sent an urgent message to his powerful relatives in Ulster who collected a large army which, with the aid of some Connachtmen, engaged the King at Cooldruman and defeated him, leaving three thousand dead on the field. King Diarmaid himself was killed in the battle, his death being brought about, according to *The Annals of Ulster*, 'through the prayers of St. Columba.'[5]

Columba, repenting the bloodshed, went to confession to St. Molaise of Innishmurray who imposed on him the penance of 'spending the rest of his life an exile on foreign soil where he should win more persons for Christ than had fallen in battle.' Columba sorrowfully departed from his monastery at Drumcliff and sailed with some monks for the west coast of Scotland where he made his great foundation on the island of Iona from which the Picts and Scots were converted to Christianity.

Columba was also a poet who played an important part in bringing about a reconciliation between Celtic mythology and Church teaching. He returned from Iona to the Convention of Druim Ceat in 575, where his spirited defence of the poets rescued them from banishment.[6] 'As a result, Ireland was in an almost unique position in the middle ages: here learning and literacy were not the preserve of the Christian clergy. As late as 1539 a formal treaty between Manus O'Donnell and O'Connor Sligo invokes the satire of the poets and excommunication by the clergy as penalties for its violation.'[7]

A number of poems attributed to St. Columba have survived, including one which refers to his sorrow at having to leave his native land. The following is a stanza from this, translated by Dr. Douglas Hyde in his *Literary History of Ireland*.

How dear to my heart is yon western land,
Is the thought of Lough Foyle where the cool waves pour,
And the Bay of Drumcliff on Culchinne's strand;
How grand was the slope of its curving shore!

11 Lissadell

The light of evening, Lissadell,
Great windows open to the south. — W. B. Yeats

In 1894 W. B. Yeats visited Lissadell when he was staying with his grandmother in Sligo. Thirty years later he looked back over one of the most turbulent periods of Irish history and, at Seville in Spain, wrote his well-known elegy in memory of the two beautiful girls who listened to his poetry and his plans for the Irish Literary Movement.[1]

The two beautiful girls were Eva and Constance Gore-Booth. Eva became the well-known poetess who wrote 'The Little Roads of Cloonagh,' and Constance, reputed to be the finest horsewoman in Ireland, became the Countess de Markievicz.

Lissadell (in Irish, 'the fort of the blind man') was once owned by a branch of the O Dálaigh (O'Daly) family, hereditary poets who were free of tribute (rent) because of their profession. In 1213 Muiredach O Dálaigh slew with an axe O'Donnell's tax-collector who angered him (Lissadell was in territory from which O'Donnell claimed tribute). He had to flee to Scotland from O'Donnell, but was later restored to favour and to Lissadell by writing poems in praise of O'Donnell.[2]

A few miles north of Lissadell is Streedagh Strand where three ships of the Spanish Armada were wrecked in 1588. One of the survivors, Don Francisco de Cuellar, was befriended by the MacClancy at Lough Melvin and by Brian O'Rourke, Prince of Breifne. He eventually returned to Spain via Scotland and wrote an account of his adventures.[3]

From Coney Island the pine woods of Lissadell can be clearly seen, framing the austere neo-classical mansion built (of Ballysadare limestone) in 1832 for Sir Robert Gore-Booth, the grandfather of Eva and Constance. The architect was Francis Goodwin of London.

Constance Gore-Booth became a rebel against the Anglo-Irish landed class into which she had been born. In 1900 she married a Polish artist, Count Casimir Dunin de Markievicz, whom she met while studying art in Paris. From 1908 she devoted her life to the freedom and welfare of the Irish poor. In 1909 she founded Fiana Eireann, a nationalist boy scout movement. She supported James Connolly in the Transport Workers' Strike of 1913, became a leader in the 1916 Rising and was sentenced to death. Her sentence was commuted to life imprisonment, but she was released in 1917. On 23 August of that year the Freedom of the Borough of Sligo was conferred on her. For the next ten years, until her death, she played a prominent part in Irish politics. In 1918 she had the distinction of being the first woman to be elected to the British House of Commons, but she never took her seat. She was Secretary for Labour in the Dáil Cabinet of 1920, and at the General Elections of 1923 and 1927 she was returned to Dáil Eireann for the Dublin South constituency.

An ardent admirer and supporter of De Valera, Countess de Markievicz found herself opposed to W. B. Yeats who had also entered politics, and who was appalled at what he regarded as the downfall of the beautiful, courageous woman who rode with the County Sligo Harriers.

> That woman's days were spent
> In ignorant good-will,
> Her nights in argument
> Until her voice grew shrill.
> What voice more sweet than hers
> When, young and beautiful,
> She rode to harriers?

34

Constance Gore-Booth, the Countess de Markievicz, died in 1927 in a hospital in a slum quarter of Dublin, among the poor, thousands of whom followed her coffin at a public funeral.

In 1895 four Barnacle Geese arrived in Lissadell. Today, the north side of Drumcliff Bay and the Lissadell Estate have one of the largest mainland flocks of Barnacle Geese in these islands. These small geese come each year to winter in Lissadell, arriving about the third week in October, after travelling up to two thousand miles from the Greenland Arctic via Iceland and Scotland. They depart again around the third week in April.[5]

12 The Metal Man

Good morning, Mr. Metal Man,
I say, How do you do?
You're looking fine in whitelead pants
And your coat of navy blue.
Pray do not say I flatter,
For I think so with my pen;
In many ways you soar sublime
O'er us, poor mortal men.

— Sligo Street Ballad[1]

The Metal Man is a gigantic statue of a sailor standing on a stone pedestal on the half-tide Perch Rock.[2] His arm points 'to where the water is deep enough for ships' (W. B. Yeats). The statue was originally intended for the Black Rock, a dangerous reef farther out in the bay, on which now stands a 'tall pale lighthouse' (Jack B. Yeats).

In May 1818 the Corporation for Preserving and Improving the Port of Dublin, known as the Ballast Board, paid the sculptor Thomas Kirk £11[3] for a small model of the Metal Man which he had exhibited in London the previous year. In May 1819 Kirk's full-sized pattern was purchased for £75; six months later a John Clark was commissioned to cast, from Kirk's pattern, four

35

metal figures at a cost of £80 each, one of the figures being destined for the Black Rock in Sligo Bay. By October 1819 a beacon tower (commissioned in 1817) had been constructed on the Black Rock by the bridge-builder Thomas Ham of Ballina. In March 1821 Sligo's Metal Man had been cast and was in storage at 'the new quay'.

At this point a sudden change occurs in the plan for the Metal Man. The shipmasters of the Port of Sligo objected to the Metal Man being placed on the new beacon tower at Black Rock. They petitioned 'the Commissioners for improving the Town and Harbour of Sligo' to convert the beacon into a proper lighthouse, and to place the Metal Man on a pedestal on the Perch Rock. Agreement to the petition was twice postponed.[4] At last, in 1822, the Metal Man was placed in his present position on the Perch Rock.[5]

Ten years later (June 1832) the Commissioners agreed to convert the beacon tower on Black Rock into a lighthouse. The work was completed in 1835. The outside spiral staircase of the lighthouse is fixed around the original tower.[6]

Where are the three 'brothers' of the Metal Man? One stands on a white pillar on Great Newton Head overlooking Tramore Bay. The destination of the other two is not known. I heard on Coney Island that one went to Australia; I heard in Rosses Point that 'a twin brother' of the Metal Man lies comfortably on his back in a garden in Dalkey. I also heard that one went to Montevideo, capital of Uruguay, and that another took the Viking route to Norway!

According to a legend recorded by the historian W. G. Wood-Martin, the Metal Man, at certain times of the year, leaves his pedestal and goes ashore to Rosses Point.[7]

From night till morn, from morn till night,
All through the weary day,
With arm outstretched you point the course

That leads to Sligo quay.
And you never think to go on strike,
Or look for rise of pay;
You never do such silly things,
You are a model man,
A great improvement I should say
On Mother Nature's plan.

13   The Metal Man's Story

I love my dear adopted land — I love it as my life;
I love it dearly as I love my children and my wife,
But who can blame me if I love old Ireland far away,
And Sligo town that lies so snug at the foot of Knocknarea.
— American Street Ballad

In the early months of 1847 a small ship called *Carrick of White Haven* sailed out of Sligo past the Metal Man. The sailing ship was filled with starving emigrants bound for Quebec, Canada. After a bitter winter crossing, it entered the wide Gulf of the St. Lawrence River.

On 28 April 1847, as the *Carrick of White Haven* was passing the Gaspesie coast on the last leg of its journey, a fierce storm struck without warning. The crew was unable to haul in the sails. The ship was wrecked on the rocks off the little fishing settlement of Cap-de-Rosiers. Most of the crew and passengers were drowned. All would have been lost but for the efforts of the fishermen living on the coast. Eighty-seven bodies were washed ashore and buried at Cap-de-Rosiers in a mass grave over which a monument was raised by the parish priest, Monsignor Quinlan, and parishioners of St. Patrick's, Montreal. In all, 187 people were lost.

The survivors settled at Cap-de-Rosiers where, today, outside comfortable homesteads in this French-Canadian fishing village, you can see letter-boxes bearing such names as Cavanagh, Dunne and O'Connor.[1]

A quarter of a century before the *Carrick of White Haven* sailed out of the port of Sligo, the Metal Man was fixed on his perch. Even then, in 1822, 'there was a constant, steady stream of emigrants' out of poverty-stricken Sligo to America. By the year 1830 'the stream may be said to have become a torrent.'[2] In the first eight months of 1831, thirty vessels sailed from Sligo under the outstretched arm of the young Metal Man, with a total of 4,495 emigrants. From January to April 1832 thirteen vessels left the port with 4,086 emigrants.

This growing exodus reflects the partial famines which struck Ireland regularly in the thirty years before the Great Famine — all warnings of the danger which existed of a total failure of the potato crop. 'In one out of every three years in the three decades before the Great Famine there was a minor famine usually caused by crop failure in some part of the country.'[3]

One half of the Irish people had no food but potatoes and no means to purchase any other. In Connacht sixty-four per cent of land holdings were under five acres, and many of them were mere plots. The rate of wages paid by the landlords was nominal, barely enough to pay the rent of a potato plot and certainly not sufficient to buy food for a family.

In 1841 there were over eight million people in the country, and the survival of this vast, impoverished population depended on the recurring yield of the potato harvest and on that alone.

The food of the poor people is potatoes, milk and herrings, with oaten bread in Summer; all keep cows, not pigs, and but a few poultry. They have an absolute belly-full of potatoes, and the children eat them as plentifully as they like. (Arthur Young on County Sligo in 1776.)[4]

In the autumn of 1845 when the new potato disease, the blight, already known in the United States and Canada, made its appearance in England and Ireland,

38

the country was filled with foreboding. The winter of that year was one of the harshest and longest in living memory. In February there were fierce gales and the country was covered in thick snow. A fever epidemic spread like wildfire through the country. Whole families were wiped out and hundreds of thousands began to move to sea ports to flee from the stricken land. At first they sailed from Liverpool to Canada and the United States, but very soon direct sailings began from Ireland. In 1847 more than one hundred thousand emigrants sailed for Canada, this being the most economic route to the United States. It is estimated that on the way at least a fifth perished of privation, disease and drowning. It was from the smaller ports like Sligo that the notorious 'coffin ships' sailed — old and overcrowded craft whose owners had been drawn into the traffic in the hope of high profits.

In 1847, over thirteen thousand people sailed from the port of Sligo. Blight struck less hard in the autumn of that year, but in 1848 it returned with full virulence. In 1849 the staggering number of 932,000 were maintained for some time in overcrowded, insanitary workhouses. By 1851 a million had perished and another million had succeeded in getting away.

Records of emigration from 'Sligo and the outposts' in the period 1847 to 1850 show that a total of 22,510 sailed past the Metal Man, bound for Canada or the United States. There is no record of the numbers who reached land.

The enforcement of the Passenger Act at small harbours was impossible — the class from which inspectors could be drawn did not exist in Ireland. Ships sailed which were overcrowded, not provided with the legal quotas of provisions and water, and dangerously antique in construction : these were the vessels that were given the name of of "coffin ships".[5]

Emigration continued after the Famine. In 1841 the population of County Sligo was 188,886. Fifty years later it was 98,013.

14 · The Wishing Chair

On Coney Island there is a huge, grey boulder with two step-like ledges. It is called St. Patrick's Wishing Chair. It stands in a wind-swept field on the north-west shore, looking out at the Atlantic Ocean. The tradition, according to generations of islanders, is that 'the Saint himself cast it down where it is. The marks left by his fingers are still pointed out, and around the stone have grown up stories of miraculous cures and miraculously fulfilled wishes, and even today anyone can, and everyone does go and sit on one of the ledges and makes a wish once a year.'[1]

Wood-Martin, writing in the last century about this 'large erratic boulder', records that 'strangers occasionally come to pray and miraculous cures follow the petitions of the faithful.'[2] Even today, visitors take the high green road to the stone Chair where they sit silently for a few minutes gazing at Black Rock Lighthouse. As I write (1976), there are Swedes and French and Germans holidaying on the island. They have all visited St. Patrick's Wishing Chair.

As I walked home the sun was low over Lissadell. I turned south into the rabbit country and rambled along the shore under Knocknarea. Overhead there were wheeling flights of plover and curlew and the air was filled with their plaintive cries. Then a turn east with the Atlantic wind behind me and a view ahead of the narrow sea channel up to Sligo Port towards which the Metal Man — a highly painted sea mark of Napoleonic times — gestures with one arm outstretched while the waters swirl about his concrete base. I went into a big field to see the Wishing Stone, a huge piece of granite with two natural step-like seats. You sit on them and wish your heart's delight, but you may only wish once a year. . . .[3]

Another Coney Island link with the Apostle is 'a delicious St. Patrick's Well where he planted his staff among the green sandhills in the south.'[4] This is near the south shore

40

beside the ruined mansion at the entrance to the island. A strange feature of this well, according to the islanders, is that a person can draw only one barrel of water at a time. When the barrel is full the well is dry. Yet if another person comes, he can fill a barrel straightaway.

15 Killaspugbrón

Killaspugbrón today is a ruined church standing on a headland a little north of Strandhill. A narrow neck of sea separates it from the south-west shore of Coney Island. The islanders have for centuries been laid to rest in the churchyard of Killaspugbrón — the mourners walking across the strand when the tide is out. The Irish for Killaspugbrón is Cill Easbuig Bróin, meaning 'The Church of Bishop Brón'.

Bishop Brón is one of the best known of St. Patrick's disciples. His church was the first to be founded by St. Patrick in Cairbre — as the Sligo region has been traditionally called (after Cairbre, the third son of Niall of the Nine Hostages). St. Patrick put the church in charge of Bishop Brón who held a special place in his affection. According to the ancient *Tripartite Life of St. Patrick*, the Saint shed a tooth which 'he gave to Bishop Brón because he was dear unto Patrick.' To preserve the relic, a handsomely-decorated wooden shrine was made. Known as Fiacal Pádraig (Patrick's Tooth), this is now preserved in the National Museum of Ireland.[1]

In the time of St. Patrick and Bishop Brón — and for long afterwards — Killaspugbrón was called Caisel-Irra. Caisel comes from the Irish word for fort (usually a stone fort) and there is evidence that an extensive stone fort existed here, the foundations of which are now buried under the sand.[2]

Experts are not agreed on the date of the existing ruins. Dr. Petrie[3] did not rule out the possibility that they belonged to the original structure erected in the time of St. Patrick. W. G. Wakeman, however, says: 'It is not in the least degree probable that any portion of the structure erected at Killaspugbrón . . . by St. Patrick remains — at least above ground. It should be remarked, however, that the existing remains, in place and style of masonry, present indications of very considerable antiquity.' [4]

O'Rorke's careful statement that, 'one may go so far as to refer it to about the eleventh century, but hardly to an earlier date,' is probably nearest the truth. [5]

16 The Cave on Carraig Mairtín

During recent visits to Rosses Point, Sligo . . . I have been so fortunate as to discover a series of implements and flakes in limestone which, by their provenance and forms, I do not hesitate to refer to the Lower Palaeolithic (Early Mousterian) period. . . .

A little more than a mile to the south of the above-mentioned site, upon Coney Island, the remains of a large cave may be seen . . . the contents have drifted out and along the coast for a distance of half a mile, and so are now found there upon the beach. These implements, two of which are remarkable examples of Lower Palaeolithic workmanship, are, as would be expected, rolled, and exhibit on their surfaces marks due to collision with other stones. . . .

In addition to an examination of the sites at Rosses Point and at Coney Island, I have carried out a close investigation of the sections of Boulder Clay visible upon the coast, and at Ballyconnell, situated 5 miles to the north-west of Rosses Point, I discovered *in situ* at a depth of 39 feet from the surface of the ground and embedded in Boulder Clay, a core, with facetting upon both platforms, and a massive flake used as a hollow-scraper, formed of limestone. . . .

From the researches I have carried out it seems clear that the specimens are of undoubtedly human origin, and of Lower Palaeolithic (Early Mousterian) types. . . .

These extracts are from an article (illustrated by photographs of the stone implements) which appeared in the scientific journal *Nature* in 1927. Within a short time after the article appeared, the Sligo sites became a focus of attention and controversy. The author of the article was archaeologist J. P. T. Burchell.[1] In effect, Burchell claimed to have pushed the dawn of human life in Ireland back about thirty thousand years.

There is abundant evidence that Ireland was inhabited in the Neolithic or New Stone Age (the age of polished stone implements): approximately 3,000–1,800 B.C. There is also evidence of man in Ireland in the Mesolithic or Middle Stone Age (when stone implements were still only chipped): approximately 10,000–3,000 B.C. It is believed that hunters crossed from Scandinavia to Britain and then, about 6,000 B.C., moved across the narrow strait between Scotland and Antrim, and spread down through the central plain of Ireland. Mesolithic tools have been found on lake shores and river banks in Roscommon, Carlow and Limerick.[2] Burchell's discoveries, if their age were proven, would push back the evidence for human habitation in Ireland from the Mesolithic Age well into the Palaeolithic or Old Stone Age. The Palaeolithic Age began with the earliest human remains found (approximately three million years ago) and ended with the recession of the ice-age glaciers about ten thousand years ago. Burchell claimed that the implements discovered by him in Sligo belonged to the Old Stone Age, and came from the early period of the Mousterian culture which developed in Western Europe some thirty or forty thousand years ago. The chief exponent of this culture was one of the best-known characters in prehistory — short and stocky Neanderthal Man.[3]

Burchell's claim was challenged from all sides. Experts had long since concluded that 'if [Palaeolithic Man] ever existed in Ireland, he has left no conclusive evidence of his presence, so far as our knowledge goes' (*Wakeman's Handbook of Irish Antiquities*).[4] This remains the view of the majority of experts today.[5] They do not regard the discoveries of Burchell as conclusive evidence of the presence of Palaeolithic Man in Ireland. In the three years following the announcement of the Sligo discoveries, over forty scientific papers were published concerning the implements and the sites. Almost all accepted that the implements were definitely human artefacts. The dispute concerned their age, the effects of glaciation in the Sligo region, and the origin of the caves or rock shelters on Coney Island and Rosses Point.[6] The following brief outline of the controversy, together with the accompanying notes, will provide the interested reader with sufficient guidelines for further study.[7]

Burchell remained adamant that his conclusions were correct, and proceeded to publish a book on the discoveries and their significance. Another archaeologist, J. Reid Moir,[8] collaborated with Burchell in writing the book which they entitled *The Early Mousterian Implements of Sligo, Ireland.*[9] When Burchell made his original announcement, Reid Moir supported him cautiously.[10] Later he gave his full support to Burchell's thesis, and their joint work is a fascinating document.

After an introduction which summarises the grounds for the widely-held opinion 'that Ireland was uninhabited by man throughout the quaternary ice age,' there is a chapter on the quaternary ice age in England which concludes with arguments for the view 'that, on *a priori* grounds traces of Palaeolithic Man are to be anticipated in Ireland.'[11] The next chapter describes the three Sligo sites in detail. Today, after half a century, the effect of sea erosion on the Coney Island cave has been negligible. In 1928 Burchell and Reid Moir wrote that it was 'a cave 50 feet wide, 4 feet high and 6 feet from back to front. The cave, which has a north-easterly aspect, was at one time 25 feet from back to front. The floor is washed at high water. It is presumed that Palaeolithic Man occupied this or some adjacent cave which has long since been washed away, at a time when the land stood higher

44

than it does at present.'

The cave in question is on Carraig Mairtín and the implements were discovered by Burchell on nearby Carraig Fhada which he accurately describes as 'a strip of beach material some 250 yards in length situated at the level of present day high tides.' [12]

The next chapter is devoted to a detailed description (illustrated by diagrams) of the method by which the implements were made, and the implements themselves are then described. There are numerous photographs and plates, accompanied by notes, illustrating the sites and the implements.

Archaeologists divide the Mousterian period into earlier and later. Remains of later Mousterian Man have been found at various sites in Europe (Germany, France, Italy and the U.S.S.R.) as well as in North Africa and Palestine. Burchell and Reid Moir claimed that the Sligo implements dated from the earlier Mousterian period.

According to some experts, Mousterian Man disappeared rather abruptly from Europe at the climax of the last glaciation.[13] It is conceivable that, as the colossal mountains of ice melted and began to move, the fertile inhabited lowlands were again covered by ice. According to Burchell and Reid Moir, something like this happened to the Sligo sites and, indeed, to the whole country. In their book they state: 'From the discovery at Ballyconnel of specimens embedded in Boulder Clay it is clear that since the makers of the Sligo implements lived, Ireland has been subjected to a glaciation.'[14] This view, they claim, is consistent with the evidence yielded by the pre-glacial caves in Keshcorran, Co. Sligo.[15]

The majority of experts, as already stated, were not convinced by Burchell and Reid Moir. Early in the debate their findings were questioned on geological grounds: and, fifteen years after the discoveries, H. L. Movius, in his authoritative work, *The Irish Stone Age*, pronounced

45

the evidence to be inconclusive, mainly because of disregard of geological data.[16] In their book, however, Burchell and Reid Moir state that an evaluation had been made of the geological evidence which was believed to be 'sound and reliable.' [17] They do not elaborate on this point; and they freely admit that a number of questions 'must be left for final solution until further and more extensive investigations have been carried out.' [18]

Perhaps, after half a century, the time has come for these further investigations using today's methods which, in addition to the study of artefacts and sites by archaeologists and geologists, call for the co-ordinated efforts of other specialists — such as botanists, zoologists and chemists — in examining the total environment of the area in which the implements were discovered. Such investigations might include (1) a new look at the caves of Keshcorran in which, says Robert Lloyd Praeger, 'a whole museum of bones was unearthed, including those of Reindeer and Arctic Lemming';[19] (2) a scientific examination of the flora on Ben Bulben which, according to Daphne D. C. Pochin Mould, 'may well be a pre-glacial relict'.[20]

Discovery and surprise are constant features of archaeology and anthropology. In 1959 and 1961, British anthropologists Dr. Louis Leakey and Dr. Mary Leakey, working in the Olduvai Gorge in northern Tanzania, pushed the dawn of of the human race back to one million eight hundred thousand years ago. In 1972 they pushed it back beyond two million years with the discovery of a human skull in Lake Turkana (Kenya). In 1974-75, American anthropologist, Dr. Donald Johanson, working in Hadar, Ethiopia, discovered the skeleton of a girl who 'laughed and cried and walked upright on the plains of northern Ethiopia three million years ago.' Johanson and his team named the girl 'Lucy'. Before this discovery, the earliest skeleton as complete as Lucy dated from no more than one hundred thousand years ago.

Beside these discoveries the claim of Burchell and Reid Moir to have pushed back the dawn of man in Ireland by thirty thousand years does not appear so startling.[21] In 1972 a discovery was made in Co. Louth which was even more surprising than Burchell's in Sligo. A flint flake was found near Drogheda on the surface of glacial gravel deposited as early as 200,000 B.C. 'It documents the existence of man in middle Palaeolithic times close to the basin of the Irish Sea.'[22]

17   Fairies and Faeryland

A little north of the town of Sligo, on the southern side of Ben Bulben, some hundreds of feet above the plain, is a white square of limestone. No mortal has ever touched it with his hand; no sheep or goat has ever browsed grass beside it. There is no more inaccessible place upon the earth. . . . It is the door of Faeryland. In the middle of the night it swings open, and the unearthly troop rushes out. All night the gay rabble sweep to and fro across the land, invisible to all. . . .

— W. B. Yeats[1]

Fairies and Faeryland are very much part of Irish folklore. This is especially so in Sligo. Discussing the quarrels and conflicts of Fairies, the historian W. G. Wood-Martin writes:

There is a fort on the edge of the cliff, close to a locality named Pollnamaddow on Coney Island; but here, in addition to the fights, an old islander avers that many years ago he saw lights in the place one night, and heard the sounds of fairy festivities; he added however that since the abolition of illicit distillation these tiny inhabitants of his island had all emigrated.[2]

Woodmartin is here referring to the western fort which overlooks the deep pool off Carty's Strand which is called Pollnamada. This fort is an earthen ring (with some stones) of the type commonly found throughout the country. Formerly regarded as ritual sites, there is now clear

47

evidence from excavation that these ring forts were enclosures or ramparts around early farmsteads. They date from the end of the late Bronze Age (500 B.C.) and historical data indicate that most of them were occupied until the end of the twelfth century, and some for much longer. The Irish for an earthen fort is *lis* (often spelled *lios*) or *rath*. The prevalence of *lis* or *rath* in townland names throughout the country indicates how numerous these forts were. Wakeman estimated that, 'notwithstanding the destructive agencies of time,' there were between twenty-eight thousand and thirty thousand raths in the whole of Ireland.[3]

These forts are often referred to as 'Fairy Forts.' In Irish folklore the Fairies or the Good People are supposed to reside in them. The Gaelic name for the Fairies is *Sidhe* (pronounced Shee), a name they have retained from the ancient days when they were regarded as gods. A single fairy is called *Siog* (pronounced sheeogue).

In her *History of Irish Fairies*, Dr. Carolyn White writes:

In Ireland two distinct fairy types exist — the trooping fairies and the solitary fairies. The trooping fairies are to be found in merry bands about the hawthorn tree or at feasts in gilded palaces. They delight in company, while the solitary fairies avoid large gatherings preferring to be left by themselves and separate from one another. The trooping fairies are the major and presiding residents of fairyland; but the solitary ones have greater interest in mortal affairs and hence are generally more familiar to us.[4]

Coney Island has many stories about the fairies and their near relatives, the mermaids. The historian Tadhg Kilgannon records a number of them: horses and machines on the rocks of Carraig Fhada at midnight; fairy nets fouling the nets of the King's boat on Martin's Night; the mirage of the big burning house; the white mermaid 'standing in the water between the nets and the shore' and then, incredibly, 'swimming or sailing against both wind and tide.' The stretch of sea off Bomore Strand (the long strand at Rosses Point) was the favourite haunt of mermaids, according to the island's King, whom Kilgannon interviewed at the beginning of this century.[5] Sheelah Kirby in *The Yeats Country* also alludes to the stories of mermaids seen by 'the Coney Island men who fished off the strand at night.' [6]

Kilgannon ends his account of the Coney Island fairies with this comment from the island's King, John McGowan, grandfather of John McGowan who now resides on the island.

Although I don't believe much myself in fairies or ghosts, I must give in that it's true, every word about the mowing machine working away on the rocks at midnight; and that the mermaid appeared to the three of us outside Bomore Strand, and that I would have caught her only for Mickey Haran. Yes, there are some queer things to be heard and seen sometimes about this place.[7]

McGowan is the great name of Coney Island. From the McGowan clan came the kings of the island, and some of its great boatmen. In 1969 the once-powerful boatman Pat McGowan died. After spending ten years assisting his father with the channel lights,[8] and twenty years as a seaman, Pat emigrated to New York where he built up his own fleet of taxis. Forty years later he returned to spend his last days on Coney Island which (he told me) 'never left my mind for a single day.'

Happily the future of the dynasty is assured in the charming and friendly family of John McGowan and his wife Margaret. Assured also is Coney Island's living link with St. Patrick and the days when the Mass bell of Killaspugbrón was heard above the Atlantic breakers on Carty's White Strand.[9]

You've kindly hearts in Coney Isle, and welcome's always there,
You'll find the clasp of friendship's hand to greet you everywhere;
Yes, true and real and honest hearts — no base deceit or guile —
O! may you thus remain for aye, dear hearts of Coney Isle.
— R. J. Milne.[10]

49

18 Knocknarea

The wind has bundled up the clouds high over Knocknarea,
And thrown the thunder on the stones for all that Maeve can say.
Angers that are like noisy clouds have set our hearts abeat;
But we have all bent low and low and kissed the quiet feet
Of Cathleen, the daughter of Houlihan.

— W. B. Yeats[1]

Crowned by Miosgán Meabha (Irish for Maeve's Cairn), flat-topped, limestone Knocknarea (1,078 feet) is one of the most memorable mountains in Co. Sligo. Yeats was haunted and inspired by its mythology. It features in seven of his poems.[2] Cathleen Ní Houlihan is one of the poetic names for Ireland. It is also the title of a famous play by W. B. Yeats which had its first public performance in 1902 with the beautiful Maud Gonne playing the title role. After the staging of this play (in St. Teresa's Hall, 36 Clarendon Street, Dublin) the Irish Literary Theatre became the Irish National Theatre.

Authorities are not agreed on the derivation of the name Knocknarea. The most usual Gaelic form is Cnoc na Rí meaning 'the Hill of the Kings.'[3] The Knocknarea Cairn, which probably covers an unopened passage grave, is said to be the tomb of Maeve, Queen of Connacht. It is rather unlikely, however, that Queen Maeve, who flourished in the first century A.D., rests beneath this massive cairn (600 feet in circumference and 34 feet high). Maeve is probably buried at Cruachan (called after Cruacha, Maeve's mother), near Tulsk, in Co. Roscommon, where she resided with her husband King Ailill.[4]

Another poem of Yeats, 'The Black Tower' has:

There in the tomb stand the dead upright.

This refers to a legend that, near the tomb of Queen Maeve on the mountain, is a smaller tomb of the warrior

King of Connacht, Eoghan Bell who, after receiving his death wound at the Battle of Sligo, which was fought between the men of Connacht and the men of Ulster in 537 A.D., commanded that he be buried upright with his red javelin in his hand and his face to the north: a gesture of heroic defiance like that of Cuchulain in tying himself to a column at the moment of death. 'Place my face to the north,' said the dying King, 'and my grave on the north side of the hill by which the Northerns pass when flying before the army of Connacht.' Both sides claimed victory in this 'terrible battle in which the water of the Garavogue River ran red with the blood of the combatants.'

There are many other legends of Knocknarea. For the reader familiar with the poetry of Yeats it will suffice to say that the Knocknarea area is 'The Land of Heart's Desire,' the setting for 'The Hosting of the Sidhe' and the scene of Oisín's meeting with St. Patrick in Yeats's version of 'The Wanderings of Oisín':

> Caoilte, and Conan, and Finn were there,
> When we followed a deer with our baying hounds,
> With Bran, Sceolan, and Lomair,
> And passing the Firbolgs' burial-mounds,
> Came to the cairn-heaped grassy hill
> Where passionate Maeve is stony-still.

At the foot of Knocknarea, in the region of Carrowmore, are the 'burial-mounds' — one of the largest concentrations of megalithic tombs in Europe. More than eighty-five tombs are said to have survived down to the nineteenth century when many were rifled by amateur archaeologists, levelled by 'improving' farmers and demolished by the opening of sand-pits.[5] The remains of thirty tombs survive, consisting of dolmens, stone circles and cairns.[6]

At the southern base of Knocknarea there is a wide, spectacular cleft or chasm called 'the Glen.' The sides are lined with trees and shrubs which give the effect of a vast open-air church. Because of its mild and moist climate there is a great luxuriance of ferns and other ground flora, particularly hart's tongue; there are also many higher plants such as bugle, ivy broomrape, and wood sanicle. The limestone walls and some of the trees are covered with incredibly beautiful mosses.

The Glen is one of the most interesting botanical areas in the North West of the country. In addition to its native vegetation, it still has many of the tropical and semi-tropical plants introduced there by the Phibbs family who lived in the once beautiful but now roofless mansion of Lisheen beneath the southern slopes of Knocknarea. Geoffrey Phibbs (1900–1957) was a recognised authority on zoology and botany, and published a number of works, including *Victorian Flower Garden* (London 1952) which is considered a standard work on the subject. Writing under the name of Geoffrey Taylor, he was a poet of considerable ability and the author of a number of prose works including *Irish Poets of the Nineteenth Century* (London, 1951), *The Emerald Isle* (London, 1952), and, as co-editor with John Betjeman, *English Love Poems* (London, 1957).

On the northern side of Knocknarea stands another roofless mansion, Rathcarrick, once the seat of the Walker family who also owned the white house now known as 'Walker's Lodge' which can be seen near Killaspugbrón as one crosses Cummen Strand to Coney Island.

19   Oisín in Tír na nOg

The story of Oisín's sojourn in Tír na nOg (the Land of Youth) is another of the great tales of Ireland. According to it Oisín (son of Fionn), the renowned hero-poet to whom the ancient bards attributed many poems still extant, survived to the time of St. Patrick — two hundred years after all the other members of the Fianna (the legend makes it three hundred years). When the Saint asked him how he had lived to such a great age, the old hero related an extraordinary story which reflects the vague belief of the ancient Irish that there was a land where people remained always youthful, suffered no disease, and lived for ever. This country was called by various names, the most common being Tír na nOg, the Land of Youth. It had its own inhabitants — fairies; but mortals were sometimes brought there, and while they lived in it, they were gifted with the everlasting youth and beauty of the fairy people themselves, and they partook of their pleasures. Tír na nOg was situated 'on the verge of the azure sea' far out in the Atlantic Ocean.

One dewy morning Fionn and the Fianna were hunting a deer when they saw a rider coming swiftly towards them from the west. It was a lovely maiden on a white steed. She wore a brown robe of silk and her yellow hair flowed far down over her robes in bright golden ringlets. She introduced herself to Fionn as Niamh of the Golden Hair, daughter of the King of Tír na nOg. 'I love your noble son, Oisín, and that is what has brought me to Ireland. I have often heard of his bravery, his gentleness and the nobleness of his person.'

'When I heard these words,' said Oisín to St. Patrick, 'and when I looked on the lovely maiden with her glossy, golden hair, I was all over in love with her. . . . I bade farewell to my dear companions, and mounted the white steed, while the lady kept her seat before me. She gave the signal and the steed galloped swiftly and smoothly towards the west, till he reached the strand; and when his gold-shod hoofs touched the waves, he made no delay, but plunged forward at once, moving over the face of the sea with the speed of a cloud-shadow on a March day. The wind overtook the waves and we overtook the wind, so that we straightaway lost sight of land.'

After many adventures on the sea, Oisín and golden-haired Niamh reached Tír na nOg where they were married in the presence of the King. 'I lived in the Land of Youth more than three hundred years,' continued Oisín to St. Patrick, 'but it appeared to me that only three years had passed since the day I parted from my friends. At the end of that time I began to have a longing desire to see my father, Fionn, and all my old companions, and I asked leave of Niamh and of the King to visit Ireland: "I will give consent, though I feel sorrow in my heart, for I fear much that you will never return to me." '

When Oisín returned to Ireland, everything seemed strangely altered. 'I saw no sign of Fionn and his host, and I began to dread that Niamh's saying was coming true. At length I came to Glenasmole[1] where a number of men were trying in vain to raise a large flat stone. I stooped forward and seized the flag with one hand; and putting forth my strength, I flung it seven perches from its place. But with the great strain the golden saddle-girth broke, and bounding forward to keep myself from falling, I suddenly came to the ground on my two feet. Instantly a woeful change came over me: the ruddy beauty of my face fled, I lost all my strength, and I fell to the earth, a poor, withered old man, blind and wrinkled and feeble.

'The white steed was never seen again. I never recovered my sight, my youth and my strength; and I have lived in this manner, sorrowing without ceasing for my gentle, golden-haired wife, Niamh, and thinking about my father, Fionn, and the lost companions of my youth.'

After an interesting and sometimes amusing discussion about the opposing qualities of pagan life and of Christianity, Oisín was baptised by St. Patrick.[2]

20 Dunán Pádraig

Dunán Pádraig, (Irish for 'Patrick's Little Fort') is a tiny island lying a short distance from the south shore of Coney Island. This little green isle always appears above high water — even in the highest spring tides. The following is the tradition associated with it, as recorded by the historian W. G. Wood-Martin:

St. Patrick, when in Sligo, resided for some time on Coney Island, and observing the need of a safe communication with the mainland, commenced a causeway, which was to connect it with Strandhill. He sent a message to his hostess, a woman named Stoney, that is Mulclohy, (hence the ancient name of the Island, Inishmulclohy), to cook a rabbit for his dinner. When, however, the saint sat down, pronouncing a blessing on the food, a gigantic cat jumped off the platter set before him. It would seem that his hostess, not having a rabbit in readiness, substituted a fine specimen of the feline tribe. St. Patrick was so disgusted at this treatment that he never resumed his work, and his ante-dinner labour is now represented by the small island styled Doonanpatrick. On taking his departure, instead of leaving a blessing on the islanders, he prayed that there might never be four of the name of Stoney (that is, sons of the same father and mother) alive at the same time to carry the remains of one of their relations to the grave.[1]

It is not surprising, therefore, that although Coney Island is still marked on the Ordnance maps as Inishmulclohy (Mulclohy's Island), the family itself died out on the island centuries ago![2]

St. Patrick had a happier experience when he requested a salmon for his meal. The well-known story is told by the historian Terence O'Rorke:

The salmon fishery of the bay is remarkable for the number and quality of the fish, and for the fact that they are in season throughout the whole year. Naturalists have not been able to account satisfactorily for this fact, but the authors of the old lives of St. Patrick ascribe the valuable peculiarity to the blessing of the Saint. The *Vita Tripartita* tells that the saint, having in his missionary rounds reached the Sligo river in the winter season, and, being greatly fatigued, and in need of refreshment, having asked a salmon of fishermen whom he met at the river, was informed by them that salmon were never taken there in the winter. They added, however, that as he desired it, they would cast the net, and, having done so, they took a fine salmon which they presented to the saint; he in return for the kindness, blessed the Sligeach, and imparted to it the privilege of yielding salmon all the year round.[3]

The inhabitants of the Sligo region, following the example of Bishop Brón, embraced Christianity wholeheartedly. A number of well-known saints were Sligonians by birth — Attracta, Fechin, Nathy and Farannan.

21   Cummen Strand and the Fourteen Pillars

The old brown thorn-trees break in two high over Cummen Strand,
Under a bitter black wind that blows from the left hand.
— W. B. Yeats

Cummen Strand is the wide, inter-tidal expanse of sand between the Sligo-Strandhill road and Coney Island. It takes its name from the townland of Cummen (the Irish means 'the little common') which is divided in two by the road to Strandhill.[1] A stream called Cummen River flows under the road and into the sea just below a ruined mansion once occupied by the Ormsby family.[2] The entrance to the ruins is on the right hand side as one goes to Strandhill, a short distance beyond Cummen River. A curious feature of these remains is 'Ormsby's Folly,' a mock structure erected to give the impression of grandeur and antiquity. The Folly served its purpose: the 1839 *Traveller's Guide to Ireland* described Cummen House as a very noble edifice, with beautiful and extensive parks, gardens, and demesnes.

Another stream called Scarden River flows on to Cummen Strand; it once powered the old Scarden Mills which have recently been demolished; their ruins are barely visible on your left as you come to the end of the short road leading to Cummen Strand and Coney Island. Coney Islanders still call this little road 'the mill road.'

A century ago the Sligo Harbour Board had before it an ambitious proposal to reclaim a large section of Cummen Strand. The proposal came from private subscribers who had commissioned a London firm of engineers (Russ and Minns) to draw up plans for the reclamation of 2,400 acres. The Harbour Board rejected the proposal because the harbour and channel would be 'injuriously affected thereby.' Whereupon a modified scheme to reclaim 900 acres was submitted in the year 1880. This too was turned down, again because of fears for the harbour which (as one of the Harbour Commissioners pointed out at the Board Meeting of February 1880) 'at present is land-locked at the highest spring tides.'[3]

Ornithologists should be pleased that the plans for reclamation fell through. Cummen Strand is now a wetland site of international importance. The species occurring in numbers of international significance is the Brent Goose. In the past three years it has been established that some of the geese arriving on Cummen Strand have set out from Melville, Bathurst and Prince Patrick Islands within the Canadian Arctic Circle. It is not uncommon to have as many as 15,000 wildbirds on Cummen Strand in the winter months. Not all of these are Brent Geese, of course: there are sizeable numbers of Mallard, Wigeon, Teal and Swan. In the months of October and November there can be as many as 2,500 Brent Geese on Cummen Strand at one time.[4]

Overlooking Cummen Strand, on a steep slope, is Cummen Wood. Originally a hazel wood, it now has an interesting variety of other native trees including holly, blackthorn, ash, willow, alder, hawthorn and spindle tree. All of these Yeats gathers together in the line:

The old brown thorn-trees break in two high over Cummen Strand.

In the late 1700's Coney Island became known as Dorrin's (or Dorren's) Island, and the strand as Dorrin's Strand. The correct spelling is Doran according to the late Owen Tweedy who was the great-great-great-grandson of George Doran who acquired the island in 1784 and began to erect the imposing building which became known as 'Island House.' [5]

In 1788 Olivia, daughter of George Doran, married Tom Meredith of Cloonamahon, a descendant of Richard Meredith, a Welshman who came to Ireland in the time of Cromwell. The dowry which Olivia Doran brought with her into the Meredith Estate was Coney Island. Though Tom Meredith lived occasionally — and died — on the island, the house and lands were regarded locally as belonging to the Doran family. On 9 March 1823, William Doran, described as 'proprietor of the island' was drowned while crossing the strand to his house. It was this drowning which eventually led to the erection of the pillars on the strand, an event recorded as follows by the historian W. G. Wood-Martin:

The work that St. Patrick abandoned [the little island Dunán Pádraig] has in later days been to some extent effected by the Grand Jury of the County.[6] The direct route to the island across the Strand is now marked by 14 pillars, built of stone, and placed in a direct line from the old Scarden Mills. The pillars are on quadrangular bases with steps, having rings strongly secured to the pillars; these have been instrumental in saving many lives, for persons overtaken by the tide may often be observed clinging to the rings or seated on the summit of a pillar, where they present a most singular appearance. A roadway is now in course of construction.[7]

The pillar rings have long since disappeared because of corrosion by the sea; the embedded remnants can be seen on the north side of each pillar. The roadway which was under construction in 1891 (when Wood-Martin was writing) replaced an older roadway, shown on a marine chart of 1859, which had disappeared in the sand. The 1891 roadway was laid at the insistence of the Coney Islanders who, in a letter to *The Sligo Champion* (11 October 1890) pointed out that 'within the last nine months no less than three lives have been lost in endeavouring to come across the dreary and dismal expanse of sand which lies between the Island and the mainland. It is in the memory of some of the oldest inhabitants of the Island that as many as twenty-eight human beings have been drowned on that strand coming to the Island.' The gravel road put down in 1891 has now subsided and, completely covered by sand, is indistinguishable from the surrounding strand.[8]

The instant one crosses the border of County Sligo one hears the voice of Yeats murmuring : "Beware that they do not drive the living imagination out of the world."

— Bryan MacMahon[9]

59

Notes on the Text

1 Sligo

1 For an account of Carlyle's visit to Sligo see *Sligo and Its Surroundings*, Tadhg Kilgannon, Sligo, 1926, pp. 99, 100.

2 *Journey Throughout Ireland During the Spring, Summer and Autumn of 1834*, Whittaker, London, 1834.

3 In the sixth century St. Lommán founded a monastery on Church Island in Lough Gill. The fire of 1416 destroyed not only the church but all the O Cuirnín manuscripts. The lineal representative of the O Cuirnín family was still living on Church Island at the time of John O'Donovan's visit in 1839. There is also a ruined medieval chapel on Gallagher's (or Cottage) Island. This was a foundation of the first half of the thirteenth century, attached to Trinity Island, Lough Cé (Co. Roscommon) where a Premonstratensian abbey was founded in 1215.

4 Innisfree (in Irish, 'the island of heather') is referred to in the *Annals of the Four Masters* under the year 1244 A.D. when it was apparently the lake dwelling of a local chieftain.

   The 'Annals of the Four Masters' (in Irish 'Annála Rioghachta Eireann') is one of the greatest sources of Irish history. The 'Annals' were compiled by Brother Michael O'Clery and his three confreres, Fearfeasa Mulconry, Peregrine O'Duigenan and Peregrine O'Clery, in the residence of the Donegal Franciscans on the River Drowes (Bundrowes, Co. Leitrim), between the years 1632 and 1636. Sligo man Fergal O'Gara, Lord of Moygara and Coolavin, commissioned the work and paid the expenses involved. The autograph copy of the 'Annals' (presented to O'Gara) is now preserved in two MSS, one in the Royal Irish Academy, Dublin, and the other in Trinity College, Dublin. The first English translation of the 'Annals' was made by Sligo-born Owen Connellan from Tireragh, Gaelic scholar and historiographer to George IV and William IV. His completed volume, entitled 'Annals of Ireland', was published in Dublin in 1846. Shortly afterwards John O'Donovan began work on a new edition and translation published in Dublin by Hodges, Smith, 1848–1851. W. B. Yeats paid tribute to the ability of the Four Masters 'to record the goodness or the badness of Irishmen and Englishmen with entire impartiality.'

61

(Commentary on Edmund Spenser quoted in *W. B. Yeats, Selected Criticism*, Edited by A. Norman Jeffares, Macmillan, London, 1964, p. 115.)

The historian Terence O'Rorke writes: 'No county in Ireland has rendered such service as Sligo in the preservation of ancient lore.' From Sligo have come such outstanding compilations as 'The Book of Lecan', 'The Yellow Book of Lecan', 'The Book of Genealogies' and 'The Book of Ballymote', a folio of five hundred pages which was compiled about the year 1391, bought from McDonagh for 140 milch cows by Hugh Duff O'Donnell in 1522, and is now in the possession of the Royal Irish Academy, Dublin. Other compilations — such as the O Cuirnín manuscripts of Lough Gill — have been destroyed or lost. For a moving account of the labours of 'the Four Masters' see *Irish Essays Literary and Historical*, Archbishop John Healy, C.T.S., Dublin, 1908, pp. 1–17. See also *The Four Masters and their Work*, Fr. Paul Walsh, Three Candles Press, Dublin, 1944; *Michael O Cléirigh and his Associates*, Fr. Brendan Jennings, O.F.M., Talbot Press, Dublin, 1936.

5 'This is the land of the quaint mountain formations and the lovely lakes; of Ben Bulben, Keshcorran and Knocknarea. . . . The Rivers Drumcliff, Easkey, Garavogue, Owenmore, Moy and Unshin meander through the plains and valleys and around the mountain bases before discharging their fish-laden waters in the broad Atlantic. . . . Within its narrow confines it possesses a wealth of interest for the antiquarian, the geologist, the botanist, the archaeologist and the historian which few areas of comparable size can equal. Mysterious monuments of prehistoric times, megalithic graves, dolmens and cairns sprinkle the countryside and leave it neck-deep in the remains of unrecorded history.' (John C. McTernan, *Historic Sligo*, Yeats Country Publications, Sligo, 1965, p. 1.)

6 In the 1770's Sligo 'exported considerable quantities of linen and butter, as well as pickled salmon to the Mediterranean' (Constantia Maxwell, *Country and Town in Ireland under the Georges*, Dundalgan Press, Dundalk, 1949, p. 228). In 1834 the chief export from Sligo was timber to the Baltic. A lot of grain, chiefly oats and wheat, was also exported. At that time the butter trade of Sligo was still booming. In one year, December 1832 to December 1833, 150,000 casks of butter were exported.

Sligo port never recovered from the restrictions of the Second

World War. Hardly a hundred vessels visit the port annually. A new era of activity is now expected with the re-opening of Ben Bulben mines from which it is planned to export barytes through the port. Already (1976) some cargoes of the ore have left the port for Norway, destined for use in drilling operations in the North Sea.

7 Cf. *The Port of Sligo*, Senator Arthur Jackson, Dollard, Dublin, 1924. It refers (p. 4) to the 'dense crowd who cheered in an enthusiastic manner' on 31 October 1831 when 'the first steam packet left the quay at Sligo.' It was of three hundred tons burden and belonged to the Glasgow Steam Shipping Company.

8 Elsinore Lodge then belonged to Yeats's cousins, the Middletons, who in 1867 purchased the whole of Rosses Point for £17,500.

9 William Butler Yeats (1865–1939) was awarded the Nobel Prize for Literature in 1923. With Lady Gregory he helped to found Ireland's National Theatre. His brother, Jack Butler Yeats (1871–1957), is regarded by many as the greatest of Irish painters (his work is in line, water-colour, coloured drawings and oils). 'Sligo was my school,' he said, 'and the sky above it' (*Jack Yeats*, T. G. Rosenthal, Purnell, Bristol, 1966, p. 2).

10 Rosses Point, five miles northwest of Sligo, is now a popular seaside resort with miles of golden strand, a championship 18-hole golf course and a thriving yacht club. Five miles west of Sligo, at the foot of Knocknarea, is Strandhill, another delightful resort with two good beaches and an 18-hole golf course.

11 Stephen Rynne, *All Ireland*, Batsford, London, 1956, p. 175.

12 *Leinster, Munster and Connaught*, Robert Hale, London, n.d., p. 252.

2 Coney Island

1 *Gathering Moss, A Memoir of Owen Tweedy*, edited by Thomas Crowe, Sidgwick and Jackson, 1967, p. vii. The extract quoted here is from a foreword contributed by Mrs. Cecil Woodham-Smith.

2 Owen Tweedy was author of *The Dublin Tweedys, By Way of the Sahara, Gathering Moss* (edited and published posthum-

ously), and of articles for *The Fortnightly Review, The Atlantic Monthly, The Daily Telegraph, The Financial Times*; he also broadcast a number of talks for the B.B.C. The extract quoted here is from *Gathering Moss*, p. 332.

3   One is a borough in Clarion County, Pennsylvania; another is a small town in Colorado; and the third Sligo is in Peel County, Ontario, Canada.

4   Though open to question on chronological grounds, this story is firmly entrenched in the folklore of Sligo, and is recorded by many writers including John C. McTernan, *Historic Sligo*, p. 37, Tadhg Kilgannon, *Sligo and Its Surroundings*, p. 211, and Owen Tweedy, *The Fortnightly Review*, March, 1950, p. 193. Kilgannon (*op. cit.*, p. 211) says that Peter O'Connor was the founder of the firm of O'Connor and Cullen, and that the captain of the *Arethusa* was a Rosses Point man. O'Connor and Cullen were timber merchants who kept their yards stocked with Canadian timber shipped across the Atlantic in their own vessels. One of their ships was the trim 260-ton *Arethusa*, built in 1854 and fitted for the carriage of passengers as well as timber. In 1876 the *Arethusa* was still on the Atlantic route. In February of that year, its skipper, Captain Carey, was washed overboard in mid-Atlantic. Terence O'Rorke (*The History of Sligo*, Vol. 1, James Duffy, Dublin, 1889, pp. 413, 414) mentions Peter O'Connor as being aboard a ship called the *Argo* in 1830 as a sort of supervisor to ensure 'humane treatment for the passengers.' The *Argo* was owned by Pat O'Connor (presumably of the same family as Peter) who in the 1820's and 1830's shipped flax from America and emigrants from Sligo. Another of Pat O'Connor's ships was called the *Belsay Castle*. The Peter O'Connor who presented the peal of bells to Sligo Cathedral a century ago (1876) was a member of this family (see *Centenary Number Sligo Champion*, 1936, p. 37).

5   The rather rare bee orchid is found on Coney Island. Mrs. Breega Murphy of Sligo, an amateur botanist, has identified nearly one hundred interesting wild flowers on Coney Island.

   Wild life on the island is not confined to rabbits. 'There are seagulls everywhere and plover and oyster-catchers and peewit and widgeon; and on the tiny heart-shaped loch which almost cuts the island in two, occasional white swans and a regular pair of herons fish solemnly all day long in the shallows' (Owen Tweedy, B.B.C. Broadcast, 1958).

6 See Ch. 20.

7 p. 54.

8 Cf. *The Curse of Cromwell, A History of the Ironside Conquest of Ireland, 1649–53*, D. M. R. Esson, Leo Cooper, London, 1971, p. 162.

9 W. G. Wood-Martin, *History of Sligo* (1603–1688), Hodges Figgis, Dublin 1889, pp. 88, 89; Cf. T. O'Rorke, *History of Sligo*, I, pp. 179, 180.

10 O'Rorke, *op. cit.*, p. 179.

11 Wood-Martin, *op. cit.*, p. 29. Though Cromwell was doubtless aware of the natural resources of the island, he was mistaken about its size. He put Coney Island down as two hundred acres in the year 1655. The Ordnance Survey put it down as 388 statute acres, 12 perches. A few hundred acres one way or the other, or indeed a few hundred people one way or the other, would not have mattered much in the days of the Cromwellian Settlement. On the area of Coney Island see John O'Donovan, *Name Books of Sligo*, Ordnance Survey, 1838, No. 118, p. 15 (which adds that three acres, three roods and sixteen perches of Coney Island, 'is water, a small lake,' a reference to the intertidal area known as Trábheadach). For interesting glimpses of the activities of the Cromwellians in Connacht, see *The Diocese of Killala*, Most Reverend Thomas McDonnell, Ballina, 1976, pp. 114 ff.
     Much work remains to be done on the Cromwellian Settlement of County Sligo. See 'The Cromwellian Settlement of County Dublin 1652–1660,' by L. J. Arnold, *Journal of the Royal Society of Antiquaries of Ireland*, Vol. 101, Part 2, 1971, pp. 146–153. For a general picture of this period of Irish history see *Cromwell in Ireland. A History of Cromwell's Irish Campaign*, Rev. Denis Murphy, s.j., Gill, Dublin, n.d., a new edition of a well-researched work originally published in 1883; *Cromwellian Ireland*, T. C. Barnard, Oxford University Press, 1975. In *Ireland Revisited*, Hutchinson, London, New York, Melbourne, n.d., p. 11, Charles Graves speaks of 'the Irish to whom Cromwell was alive yesterday.' This is hardly an exaggeration, certainly for the west of Ireland where 'the curse of Cromwell' is engraven more deeply on folk memory than even the Great Famine. In 'The Cromwellian Settlement of Sligo' in *Sligo and its Surroundings*, Tadhg Kilgannon quotes Froude,

the English historian : 'He (Cromwell) regarded himself as dealing rather with savage beasts than with human beings, and when he tracked them to their dens he strangled the cubs and rooted out entire broods. . . . The treatment had this disadvantage — that it must be carried out to the last extremity, or it ought not to be tried at all. The dead do not come back; and if the mothers and babies are slaughtered with the men, the race gives no further trouble; but the work must be done thoroughly; partial and fitful cruelty lays up only a long debt of deserved and ever-deepening hate. . . . In justice to the English soldiers, however, it must be said that it was no fault of theirs if any child of that generation was allowed to live to manhood' (p. 42). On the Cromwellian campaign see also *A History of Ireland*, Edmund Curtis, Methuen, London, 1973, pp. 243 ff.

12 McTernan, *Historic Sligo*, p. 37.

13 Before crossing overland to Coney Island, one should be certain that the tides are favourable. *Sligo Tide Table* is published yearly by the Sligo Harbour Commissioners and is available in the town bookshops. The overland route to the island is signposted on the main road from Sligo to Strandhill.

14 B.B.C. Broadcast, 1958.

15 'One child born on the island was enough to keep that school open,' declared Katie Haran authoritatively, as she pointed to the little school-house with broken windows and missing slates. Her sister, Mrs. Mary Leyden, was the last teacher on the island. The school, which was built in the 1870's, managed to stay open until July 1940. Katie Haran is blessed with 'total recall.' Her store of history and folklore is limitless, and she is always ready to share it, embellished with amazing detail. She listed for me the principal island names in the first quarter of this century : McGowan, Haran, Ward, Carty, Feeney, Flannery and Flood. In this period some came to reside on the island : school-teachers like Miss Rennick and Mrs. Egan; retired folk like the Lloyds and Owen Tweedy who lived in the island's holiday 'lodges'; people like Sidney Tully from Glasgow who lived on the island 'while putting in the gas in Sligo town,' and a Mr. Moyes, also from Glasgow, who 'installed the gas' in the island's lighthouses. Mr. Tully lived in the then lovely 'Ivy Lodge' beside Katie's own cottage. The

Lodge, now in ruins, was built by the Merediths to take the overflow of summer visitors from 'Island House,' the now deserted mansion facing Knocknarea and Cummen Strand.

In summer, the island had a large holiday population. Families came from as far away as Elphin and Ballyfarnon, each bringing a horse and cart laden with beds, clothes and provisions for a month. One of the houses was known as 'the Boyle house' because a family from Boyle came there every year. Another was known as 'the Geevagh house'. Near Katie Haran's cottage, on the shore side of the road, can still be seen an old 'bath house' where visitors could have hot or cold sea-water baths. Some came for a holiday and stayed for the rest of their lives. Connacht Ranger and Boer War Veteran, Leo McDonald of Boyle, came for two weeks' holiday and stayed for twenty-six years. Johnny Conway from Maugherow came for some fishing and stayed for thirty-five years. 'It's like Tír na nOg,' said Michael James Ward, 'time stands still on Coney Island.'

16 In 1958 Owen Tweedy told B.B.C. listeners in a radio talk : 'Coney Island has lots of bramble hedges and by September they are laden with fine juicy blackberries, and in quite a short afternoon I can easily pick two porringers full. Last September I made thirty pounds of real good bramble jelly. . . . All round our shores we have marvellous beaches and they have millions of the loveliest shells, and all with names of their own — island names . . . whites and greens, reds and yellows, blues and pinks, browns and orange. . . .'

17 *Islands of Ireland*, Donal McCormack, Osprey, Wallop, Hampshire, 1974, p. 34.

'Is there anything else from the old days?' I asked eighty-year-old Michael James Ward one night at a 'high tea' celebrating the Stations which were held in his house that day. 'Card-playing was a great pastime,' he said, 'we were always playing cards for turkeys and geese.'

It was also a great island for song and music and dancing. Michael James himself played the violin and accordeon; Katie Haran played the organ — she still has it in her cottage; Katie's sister, Mary (the teacher), played the violin and piano; Tessie McGowan and Annie Carty played the accordeon. Coney Island was well represented in the Rosses Point Choir which 'took first prize nearly every year in Sligo Feis

Ceoil.' From her files Katie Haran once showed me a colourful certificate dated April 1928 and signed by Mary Gore-Booth and Madeline Wynne testifying that 'Miss Katie Haran won first prize at Sligo Feis Ceoil with Rosses Point Country Choir.' The conductor of the choir in those days was Mrs. McMahon who, as the former Miss Conboy, was appointed school-teacher on the island in 1906 (in succession to Miss Mitchell).

One evening Michael James showed me a colourful poster advertising 'The Coney Island Amateur Dramatic Club' which, during the 1920's, staged its plays all over County Sligo — Rosses Point, Strandhill, Carraroe, Beltra, Carney, Conway's Cross, Drumcliff, Grange, Geevagh, Kilmacowen. . . .

'Our producer was Tom Meehan. We rehearsed in Flood's loft where we had a stage and all. Katie Haran and Tessie McGowan and myself and many others were in the Dramatic Club. We were on the road in Jack Byrne's taxi all hours of the night. . . .'

One October evening in 1970 Michael James said to me: 'I haven't seen Jack Byrne for years.' Within ten minutes we were speeding across the dry strand by car. Jack was then living with his sons in Strandhill (he has since died). The two veterans, portly and similar in appearance, laughed heartily at their adventures. Their most memorable story concerned the foggy night when Jack's car got stuck on the strand. After leaving the Dramatic Club's members on the island in the early hours of the morning, Jack lost the direction of the Pillars on the return journey and the car got lodged in soft sand near Dunán Pádraig. The islanders, who had seen the lights of the car going off course, rushed to his assistance with spades and planks. They freed the car and pushed it back to the Pillars just as the incoming tide was beginning to cover the strand.

3   The Church Towers

1   *Mythologies*, Macmillan, London, 1971, p. 177.

2   This is O'Rorke's view (*History of Sligo*, I, pp. 32 ff.), and the weight of evidence, as well as present-day historical opinion, favours this view.

3   O'Rorke, *op. cit.*, pp. 156, 157. Within a short period, certainly before the century was out, the Dominicans were back in town, and their association with Sligo has continued to the present day.

4 Bishop Charles Tyndall, *The Ancient Parish and Church of St. John the Baptist, Sligo*, Sligo, 1962, p. 2.

5 'The ruin consists of a nave and a choir with a central tower in a good state of repair. For centuries visitors have marvelled at the richness and variety of the altars, the splendour of the carvings and groinings and the artistic ornamentations of the beautiful fifteenth-century east window. Sligo Abbey, an interesting remnant of other days is magnificent even in ruins' (John McTernan, *Historic Sligo*, p. 50). For concise but good descriptions of the remains of the Abbey see *The Shell Guide to Ireland*, Lord Killanin and Michael V. Duignan, Ebury Press, London, 1967, pp. 426, 427; *The Monasteries of Ireland*, Daphne D. C. Pochin Mould, Batsford, London, 1976, p. 176; *Sligo and Its Surroundings*, Tadhg Kilgannon, pp. 116–126.

6 Cf. *Sligo Cathedral Centenary Volume*, edited by Father Cyril Haran, Sligo, 1976.

7 Cf. Tyndall, *op. cit.* Cassels died in Carton House and is buried in the Protestant Church at the gate of Maynooth College.

8 *Arthur Young's Tour in Ireland*, edited by Arthur Wollaston Hutton, George Bell and Sons, London and New York, 1892, Vol. I, p. 238. Arthur Young (1741–1820), author of numerous treatises on English agriculture and economy, is remembered chiefly for the accounts of his travels in France and Ireland. From 1776 to 1779 he toured Ireland and the fascinating account of his travels is contained in the edition quoted here. He was in Sligo in August 1776.

4 Ben Bulben

1 In 1946 Yeats's body was brought home from the Chapel cemetery of Roquebrune on the French Riviera near Cap Martin (where the ailing poet spent the last two months of his life) and re-interred at the foot of Ben Bulben in the graveyard beside Drumcliff Church where his great-grandfather, Reverend John Yeats, was rector (1811–1846). Ben Bulben is often referred to in Yeats's writings, including five of his poems.

2 The highest peak in the Ben Bulben range is Truskmore (2,113 feet) on the summit of which stands a transmitting station and mast of Irish television erected there in 1962.

3   Among the plants on Ben Bulben are : the fringed sandworth, the clustered alpine saxifrage, the chickweed wintergreen, mountain avens, cushion pink yellow mountain saxifrage, green spleenworth, and holly fern; on the lower grounds you will find Canadian blue-eyed grass and the maidenhair fern (also found in the limestone chinks). Cf. *The Way That I Went*, Robert Lloyd Praeger, Allen Figgis, Dublin, 1969, p. 145; *The Mountains of Ireland*, D. D. C. Pochin Mould, Gill and Macmillan, Dublin and London, 1976, p. 53.

4   Barytes, which is composed chiefly of barium sulphate, is used in many industries including the production of chemicals and the manufacture of paints. Ben Bulben barytes has been mined intermittently since 1858 when a Mr. Williams transported the ore using a donkey-cart to Gleniff, then carted it to Mullaghmore from where it was shipped to Liverpool. The development of petroleum exploration has increased the demand for barytes. Its high specific gravity, combined with its chemical stability and lack of magnetic properties, makes barytes very suitable as a weighting additive in rotary well drilling fluids.

In other respects Ben Bulben is interesting geologically. I have watched the delight of young students of Summerhill College discovering fish and shell fossils near the summit, and later proving in their science projects that Ben Bulben was once under water — a fact already well known in the time of their grandfathers. Nearly a century ago standard manuals on geology (such as Edward Hull's and G. Henry Kinahan's) were quoted in O'Rorke's *History of Sligo* as proof 'that the Benbulben group of hills lay for ages at the bottom of the ocean, and that, vast as these ranges are, they are composed in large measure, like the coral islands of the South Sea, of fossil shells and shell fish' (Vol. I, pp. 12, 515).

5   The cave (or 'bed') of Diarmaid and Gráinne, located near the summit of a peak in the Gleniff range (not far from the barytes mines) has long been an attraction for local and visiting hill climbers.

6   The Irish version of this epic (Tóraíocht Dhiarmada agus Ghráinne, Nessa Ní Shé a chuir in eagar, Longman, Brún agus O Nualláin, Baile Atha Cliath, 1971) is on the Leaving Certificate Course for students of the Irish language. For others, one of the best translations is that of P. W. Joyce in his *Old Celtic Romances*, Talbot Press, Dublin, 1961. It is from

this work, pp. 186–236, that I have made the summary of the story which is given in the following chapter.

5 The Pursuit of Diarmaid and Gráinne

1 I am indebted to my nine-year-old niece, Olivia Finnegan, for drawing my attention to the fact that the story of Fionn and the Salmon of Knowledge forms part of the Primary School Fourth Class Reader, *Sraith na Cainte*, Leabhar G, le Seán O Finneadha, Comhlacht Oideachais na hEireann, Baile Atha Cliath, 1976, pp. 45 ff.

2 There is hardly a region in Ireland which has not got a tradition and a spot (usually called 'the bed of Diarmaid and Gráinne') associated with the famous lovers. *The Shell Guide to Ireland* mentions many of these regions.

3 Diarmaid had two spears, the great one called Ga Dearg (red javelin) and the small one called Ga Buidhe (yellow javelin); he had also two swords, the Móraltach (great fury) and the Beagaltach (little fury). These spears and swords he got from Manannán Mac Lir and Aonghus an Bhrogha. He carried the great spear and sword in affairs of life and death; and the smaller weapons in adventures of less danger.

4 Diarmaid and Gráinne had their dwelling-place at Keshcorran, four miles southeast of Ballymote, Co. Sligo. Keshcorran is a mountain (1,183 feet) which affords wide and splendid panoramas. It has a great cairn on its summit, and scattered on its slopes are seventeen small caves, one of which is called 'the Cave of Cormac Mac Airt'. The tradition is that Cormac, who was the father of Gráinne, was reared here by a she-wolf. Not surprisingly, therefore, Gráinne chose Keshcorran for her rath. Diamaid and Gráinne had four sons and one daughter.

6 The Bay to the West

1 By David W. Bone, Duckworth, Covent Garden, 1910, p. 281.

2 For access to a first edition of *The Brassbounder* and other rare books I am indebted to Miss Nora Niland, Sligo County Librarian and Curator of Sligo County Museum. In the days of sail, a ship's apprentice was ironically called a Brassbounder because, on his first voyage, he came aboard in a brass-bound uniform which was very soon discarded for more workaday

clothes. *The Brassbounder* has been reprinted a dozen times, twice in Penguin Paperback editions (Balding and Mansell, London, 1942, 1949).

3 T. W. Moody, 'Fenianism, Home Rule and the Land War,' *The Course of Irish History*, edited by T. W. Moody and F. X. Martin, Mercier Press, Cork, 1967, p. 279.

4 Until recently there was some doubt about the fate of the vessel *Erin's Hope*. On 20 July 1976, *The Irish Times* reported that a Kilmore Quay trawler had picked up some of its wreckage. The Maritime Institute of Ireland, however, says that she sailed back to New York after 'she put 31 of her passengers ashore at Helvick' (*The Irish Times*, 29 July 1976). Two of the passengers were Colonel John Warren and Colonel Augustine E. Costello (Dr. Mark F. Ryan, *Fenian Memories*, Gill, Dublin, 1946, p. 15). A booklet entitled *The Cruise of the Erin's Hope*, was published by Michael O'Mullane in Dublin in 1916.

7 The Little Sailing Boats

1 *Sligo*, Jack B. Yeats, Wishart, London, 1930, pp. 12, 13.

2 Michael James Ward's own boat was a yawl. 'The yawl is better,' he explained, 'when you are running before a sea, and better for sailing. I won sailing races with my own boat *Agnes*, and another boat *Mary*; and I won on Lough Gill against the pick of the gentry.'

It was with oars, however, that the Coney Islanders excelled. There seemed to be no end to the feats performed by Dan and Martin McGowan, and the Harans and the Cartys, in those square-sterned four-oared fishing boats, the lonesome remnants of which can be seen near the pier on the island. In John McGowan's on the island there is a plaque dated 1921 commemorating the 'members of Coney Island Boat Club' who in that year were 'champions of Sligo Bay' in races for yawls and square-sterned boats. The yawl crew were: Patrick and John Haran, Daniel and Martin McGowan, and James Kilgallan — all Coney Islanders except Kilgallan who was a Rosses Point man. The square-sterned crew were: Daniel and Patrick McGowan, Patrick and Joseph Haran, and Michael James Ward — all Coney Islanders. In the 1930's Michael James himself was 'put on' the organising committee of the Annual

Regatta at Rosses Point — without prejudice, however, to his right to compete in races.

3 *History of Sligo*, (1691–1891), Hodges, Figgis, Dublin, 1892, p. 390.

4 *The Yeats Country*, Sheelah Kirby, The Dolmen Press, Dublin, 1969, p. 35. The poet's grandfather, William Pollexfen, survived. Yeats's account of the shipwreck is in *Autobiographies*, Macmillan, London, 1961, pp. 12, 13.

5 *The Sligo Champion*, Sligo, June and July, 1880.

8 The Seagulls and the Mackerel

1 Owen Tweedy, B.B.C. Broadcast, 1958.

9 Dead Man's Point

1 *Mythologies*, p. 191.

2 Quoted by Sheelah Kirby in *The Yeats Country*, p. 36.

3 *History* (1691–1891), pp. 334, 335.

4 Sheelah Kirby, *The Yeats Country*, p. 37.

5 Elsinore Lodge, now rapidly falling into ruin, should be preserved not only for its Yeatsian and other associations, but because, in its architecture and setting, it forms an interesting feature of the shoreline at Rosses Point. It has been immortalised by Yeats, writing of his contemporary, Henry Middleton, an eccentric who lived alone at Elsinore where he kept Jersey cows and peacocks on the green before the house :

> My name is Henry Middleton,
> I have a small demense,
> A small forgotten house that's set
> On a storm-bitten green.

Elsinore would make an ideal museum and art gallery for exhibits dealing with Sligo Bay and the region around it.

10 Drumcliff

1 An Irish monk of those days, listening thankfully to the howling of the storm at night, wrote this on the margin of his

73

manuscript (the translation is by Liam de Paor, *The Course of Irish History*, p. 93):

> The wind is rough tonight
> tossing the white-combed ocean;
> I need not dread fierce Vikings
> crossing the Irish sea.

It was not until the Battle of Clontarf in 1014 that the power of the Vikings was finally broken.

2 Hazel woods were a feature of this region during the centuries when Ireland was heavily wooded. At the beginning of the seventeenth century one-eighth of the country was still forested. During the seventeenth and eighteenth centuries Irish woods were ruthlessly exploited — without replacement — for iron-smelting, shipbuilding, and the staves of casks for wine. In 1625 it was said that all French and Spanish wine was casked in Irish wood. According to some, Drumcliff means 'the ridge of the baskets' (Druim Chliabh).

3 'The chief object of interest at Drumcliff is a magnificent cross. . . . The beautiful work of Celtic art, though not nearly so large as several other examples of its class, exhibits upon its surface a wealth of carving illustrative of scripture history or of passages in the history of the locality. Several of its panels contain interlacing patterns of most curious and intricate design, each of which would form a study in itself.' W. F. Wakeman in 'The Tourist's Picturesque Guide to Ireland', *circa* 1880. For a detailed description of the cross, see Woodmartin, *History of Sligo* (1603–1688), pp. 299–303.

4 A fragmentary copy of this Latin Psalter, called the Cathach, is now preserved in the Library of the Royal Irish Academy, Dublin. It has been traditionally looked upon as the copy made by Columba in his own hand. It 'is paleographically dated to the sixth century and may indeed have been written by him' (Francis J. Byrne, 'The Ireland of St. Columba,' *Historical Studies V*, edited by J. L. McCracken, Bowes and Bowes, London, 1965, p. 37). It shows the Irish style of writing before it was subjected to seventh-century continental influence. The word 'cathach' meant 'battle-book' or 'battle relic' which a chief brought into battle with him to ensure victory. The fragmentary copy of the Psalter attributed to St. Columba was the 'cathach' or 'battle-book' of the O'Donnells until the

74

seventeenth century. Some scholars believe that the famous Book of Kells is associated with scribes of the school of Columba, and that it was painted at the monastery of Iona from which it was taken to Kells after Iona was plundered by the Vikings (see note 6).

5   Cf. *Early Christian Ireland*, Máire and Liam de Paor, Thames and Hudson, London, 1958, p. 48.

6   Cf. Francis J. Byrne, *op. cit.*, p. 37 ('the intercession of the saint rescued the poetic order from extinction'). For an excellent account of St. Columba and his work see *Ireland, Harbinger of the Middle Ages*, Ludwig Bieler, Oxford University Press, London, 1963, pp. 65 ff.

Before his exile Columba had founded many monasteries besides Drumcliff, including Durrow monastery in the midlands and one at Derry (the city is still called, in Irish, Doire Colmcille). For Columba, the monastic scholar *par excellence* was the scribe. He himself and Baithín, who succeeded him as abbot at Iona, laid the foundation of a scribal art which later became one of the greatest glories of Irish monasticism. As already stated, some believe that the Book of Kells was written and painted at the monastery of Iona. This extraordinary manuscript, which marks the culmination of early Irish art, is now preserved in the Library of Trinity College, Dublin. Even before the mutilation which resulted in the missing leaves at the beginning and end, it was an unfinished work, probably because of the disaster which befell Iona and many Irish monasteries at the end of the eighth century (see 'The Beginnings of Christianity,' An tAthair Tomás O Fiaich, *The Course of Irish History*, pp. 61–75).

> In 795, long low ships, with patterned sails, appeared from the ocean and ran their prows up on the beach. From them came helmeted warriors, armed with heavy swords and iron spears, who ransacked and burned the little churches of the monastic village [of Iona], searching for the jewelled shrines and other ornaments of the altars. Raiders were back again in 801, and yet again in 806, when they murdered no less than sixty-eight of the monks. After this visitation the abbot, Cellach, moved to Ireland with the survivors, carrying with him the precious relics of Colum Cille. He was given land at Kells in the territory of the southern Uí Néill, where he founded a new monas-

75

tery. One can imagine the Book of Kells, its ornamentation cruelly interrupted by the murderous raids, being carried back to the home country and housed with other valuables and relics in the building constructed at that time which is now known as Colum Cille's House at Kells. In gospel books as such the raiders had no interest, for they were illiterate, and pagans. (Liam de Paor, 'The Age of the Viking Wars', *The Course of Irish History*, p. 92.)

On the Book of Kells see *The Book of Kells.* Reproductions from the Manuscript in Trinity College, Dublin. With a Study of the Manuscript by Françoise Henry, Thames and Hudson, London, 1974; *The Book of Kells.* A Selection of Pages Reproduced with a Description and Notes by G. O. Simms, The Dolmen Press, Dublin, 1976. On pre-Viking Ireland see *Ireland before the Vikings*, Gearóid Mac Niochaill, Gill and Macmillan, Dublin and London, 1972.

7   Francis J. Byrne, 'Early Irish Society', *The Course of Irish History*, p. 60. There are variations in details of the story of St. Columba. According to one, it was the High King who caused the death of Curnán while he was under Columba's protection. Another says that it was St. Lasrán, abbot of Devenish, who ordered Columba to go into perpetual exile. In fact, Lasrán or Lasren (Lasarianus in Latin) was another name for Molaise of Inishmurray who founded a monastery on the island of Devenish. See *St. Columba*, N. K. Chadwick, Lesslie Newbigin, T. Ralph Morton, The Iona Community Publishing Department, Glasgow, 1963; 'Columba and Other Irish Saints in Scotland', Marjorie O. Anderson, *Historical Studies V*, pp. 26–36. For those with a knowledge of Irish, a simple account of St. Columba in Sligo and of the general history of Sligo County will be found in *Stair na gCondae, Sligeach*, An tAthair Micheál O Flanagáin, Oifig an tSoláthair, Baile Atha Cliath, 1944. An informative source on Drumcliff and on Sligo generally is *Letters of O'Donovan and Others, Containing Information Relative to the Antiquities of the County of Sligo collected during the Progress of the Ordnance Survey.* For Drumcliff see pp. 31–34.
      One of the great mapping projects of the nineteenth century was the Ordnance Survey which undertook the surveying and mapping of the boundaries of townlands and individual fields, and the recording of such features as rivers, streams, roads and

even houses. County Sligo was surveyed in 1837 and the findings were published in 1838 on six-inch maps (in 1887 the government ordered the production of sets of twenty-five-inch plans which now form the basic scale for all Ordnance Survey publications). Two valuable by-products of the Ordnance Survey were the vast amounts of historical and antiquarian information collected under the direction of the Irish scholar, John O'Donovan, who was commissioned to standardise Irish place-names. The information relating to County Sligo is contained in the 'Ordnance Survey Name Books, Sligo' (two volumes) and the 'Ordnance Survey Letters' (one volume). Much of the work of editing these papers (which have not yet been published) was done under the direction of Father Michael O'Flanagan (1876–1942), the Elphin patriot priest who was educated at Summerhill College, Sligo, and, after his ordination in 1900, taught in Summerhill for four years. He played a prominent role in the establishment of the first Dáil Eireann in which he led the prayers at the inaugural session in 1919.

11 Lissadell

1 'In memory of Eva Gore-Booth and Constance Markievicz.'

2 The story of Muiredach O Dálaigh of Lissadell killing Fionn O Brollagháin is told in the *Annals of the Four Masters* which record that the axe used by the poet was extraordinarily sharp, one blow of it sufficing to finish the unfortunate tax-collector! For an account of the O Dálaigh poets (who originated in Co. Westmeath) see *Westmeath Authors*, Marian Keaney, Longford-Westmeath Joint Library Committee, 1969, pp. 144, 145.

3 A translation of his story entitled 'Adventures in Connaught and Ulster' was published in 1897 (Hugh Allingham, London). For information on the Spanish Armada see *Graveyard of the Spanish Armada*, T. P. Kilfeather, Anvil Books, Tralee, 1967; *The Spanish Armada*, Michael Lewis, Pan Books Ltd., London, 1960; 'Armada Losses on the Irish Coast', *The Irish Sword*, 1956; 'The Technology of the Spanish Armada', Dr. Seán O'Donnell, *Technology Ireland*, Vol. 7, January 1976, pp. 32–37; *The Spanish Armadas*, Winston Graham, Collins, London, 1972 (for a good summary of Francisco de Cuellar's adventures see pp. 160–165).

4 Her family owned 31,774 acres (cf. McTernan, *Historic Sligo*, p. 56). See *Constance de Markievicz*, Jacqueline Van Voris,

The University of Massachusetts Press, 1967; *Constance, Countess de Markievicz*, Seán O Faoláin, Jonathan Cape, London, 1934.

5 Cf. *Barnacle Geese*, Forest and Wildlife Service, 22 Upper Merrion Street, Dublin; *The Atlas of Breeding Birds in Britain and Ireland*, J. T. R. Sharlock, published jointly by British Trust for Ornithology and Irish Wildlife Conservancy, Hertfordshire, 1976; *A List of the Birds of Ireland*, Robert Ruttledge, National Museum of Ireland, Dublin, 1975.

The name 'Barnacle Geese' owes its origin to the old belief that these birds grew from the shellfish of the same name. For this reason they were, in many areas, classed with fish and eaten on Fridays.

In 1971 the Minister for Lands made a Game Birds Protection Order prohibiting the killing or taking of game birds and wildfowl in this area, which is now designated a Wildfowl Sanctuary. The ministerial order was intended primarily to safeguard the Barnacle Geese at their largest and most accessible mainland haunt.

12   The Metal Man

1 For a printed copy of this ballad of 1902 I am indebted to Mr. John McMeekin, Sligo Harbour Master. There are five stanzas in the ballad. The one quoted here is the first, and this chapter will conclude with the final stanza.

2 The Metal Man is twelve feet high and weighs seven-and-a-half tons.

3 £11 7s. 2d., to be precise. For information on the Metal Man and Black Rock Lighthouse and for sending me a copy of 'A Short History of the Commissioners of Irish Lights', I am indebted to Mr. M. P. L. Costello of the Commissioners of Irish Lights, Dublin.

4 One reason seems to have been that the Inspector employed by the Sligo Town and Harbour Commissioners favoured Dead Man's Point instead of Black Rock for a lighthouse.

5 A navigational note in Alexander Nimmo's chart of Sligo Harbour, published in 1821, refers to 'the Perch Rock on which there is an Iron Statue close to the starboard hand.' Since the tenders for the erection of the pillar on Perch Rock

'upon which is to be fixed the Metal Man' did not appear until 7 January 1822 (cf. Wood-Martin, *History* 1691–1891, p. 224) either the Nimmo chart anticipated the placing of the Metal Man, or the chart containing the navigational note was not printed until after the pillar was erected in 1822. On 5 September 1825 the Commissioners resolved to have the Metal Man painted; and ever since he has appeared in smart nautical attire. In 1908 a light was first put in front of him.

6 Two panniers were added in 1863 as extra accommodation, and the lantern was reduced in height in 1934 when the keepers were withdrawn and the light was made unwatched. The panniers were removed a few years ago.

7 *History of Sligo* (1691–1891), p. 224. I am indebted to Mr. John McMeekin, Sligo Harbour Master, for giving me a copy of the interesting and informative *Short History of Sligo Harbour* (unpublished), Office of Sligo Harbour Master, Sligo, c. 1950.

13   The Metal Man's Story

1 A good account of this tragedy appeared in an article (illustrated by a photograph of the monument at Cap-de-Rosiers) by Brendan Gillen in *The Sligo Champion*, 28 January 1972. Mr. Gillen, a native of Sligo, resides in Toronto, Canada.

2 Wood-Martin, *History of Sligo* (1691–1891), p. 88.

3 Timothy P. O'Neill, 'The Catholic Church and Relief of the Poor 1815–45', *Archivium Hibernicum*, XXXI, 1973, p. 132. Cf. also T. P. O'Neill in *Social Life in Ireland 1800–45*, edited by R. B. McDowell, Cultural Relations Committee of Ireland in association with Radio Eireann, Dublin, 1957, pp. 43–56; *Ireland Before the Famine 1798–1848*, Gearóid O Tuataigh, Gill and Macmillan, Dublin and London, 1972.

4 *Arthur Young's Tour In Ireland*, vol. 1, p. 238.

5 *The Great Hunger, Ireland 1845–9*. Cecil Woodham-Smith, Hamish Hamilton, London 1962, p. 216. See also *The Great Famine, Studies in Irish History 1845–52*, edited by R. Dudley Edwards and T. Desmond Williams, Browne and Nolan, Dublin, 1956, which states that 'in Sligo crowds of starving men and women would gather in the turnip fields and scramble for the turnip-cuttings left by the harvesters' (p. 399). According to a

tradition which is still strong in the Maugherow area, Co. Sligo, at least one 'coffin ship' existed before the days of the Great Famine. It was called the *Pomano* (according to some the correct name was the *Pomania*). Having set out, apparently from Raughley, with evicted emigrants, it sank within sight of land with a total loss of life. I recently heard a man from Raughley chanting the plaintive ballad in which the tradition, dating from the 1830's, is enshrined.

> The ship she was a rotten one,
> The truth to you I tell;
> They struck her on the Corraun Rock
> Right under Lissadell.
>
> From the parish of Drumcliff
> Right back to Maugherow
> Many's the pleasant day we spent
> In the handling of the plough.
>
> Our rent was paid,
> We were not afraid
> That from home we'd have to go.
> We were forced to yield
> And quit the field
> And board the Pomano.

On post-Famine Ireland see *Ireland Since the Famine*, F. S. L. Lyons, Fontana-Collins, 1976.

14   The Wishing Chair

1   Owen Tweedy in 'St. Patrick's Coney Island', *The Fortnightly Review*, March, 1950, p. 191.

2   *History of Sligo* (1691–1891), p. 383.

3   Owen Tweedy, *Gathering Moss*, p. 318.

4   Owen Tweedy, 'St. Patrick's Coney Island', *The Fortnightly Review, loc. cit.*

15   Killaspugbrón

1   For relevant extracts (in translation) of 'The Tripartite Life of St. Patrick' see Wood-Martin, *History of Sligo* (1603–1688), pp. 294–298. For a good account of Bishop Brón and the

foundation of his church see O'Rorke, *History of Sligo*, I, pp. 428 ff. See also W. F. Wakeman, 'Architectural peculiarities of some ancient churches in County Sligo', *R.S.A.I. Journal*, 1886, Vol. 17, pp. 43–54.

2 The derivation of Irra is not known for certain. Though Caisel-Irra was not used as a place name in the time of O'Donovan (*Ordnance Survey Letters, Sligo*, p. 22, sect. 63), Cuill Irra, in English Coolera, was and still is a living place name (see chapter entitled 'Coolera' in O'Rorke, *History*, Vol. I, pp. 417–439).

3 *Inquiry into the Origin and Uses of the Round Towers of Ireland*, p. 178, quoted by O'Rorke, *op. cit.*, p. 431.

4 Wakeman, *op. cit.*, quoted by Wood-Martin, *loc. cit.*

5 O'Rorke, *op. cit.*, p. 431.

16   The Cave on Carraig Mairtín

1 'Discovery of Stone Implements of Lower Palaeolithic Age in Ireland'. J. P. T. Burchell, *Nature, A Weekly Illustrated Journal of Science*, Vol. 120, 20 August 1927, p. 261.

2 Cf. 'Prehistoric Ireland', G. F. Mitchell, *The Course of Irish History*, pp. 30–42; 'Archaeology Mesolithic', G. F. Mitchell, *Encyclopedia of Ireland*, Allen Figgis, Dublin, 1968, pp. 65–67.

3 The terms 'Mousterian' and 'Neanderthal' (and many other such terms) come from archaeological sites; the former from Le Moustier in France; the latter from a site in the valley of the Neander River in Germany where human remains were excavated in 1856. Cf. *Prehistoric and Primitive Man*, Andreas Lommel, New York, Syndey, Toronto, 1976, pp. 14 ff.; *Encyclopaedia Britannica*, Vol. 17, under 'Paleontology'; *Prehistoric Man*, Robert J. Braidwood, Oceana Publications, New York, 1961; *The Irish Stone Age*, H. L. Movius, Cambridge, 1942; *The Archaeology of Ireland*, Peter Harbinson, Bodley Head, London, 1976. Younger readers should be referred to the relevant sections in their 'books of knowledge': for example, 'Prehistoric Man' in *The New Book of Knowledge*, Grolier, New York; 'The Ice Ages', *ibid.*; 'A New Look at Neanderthal Man' in *Our Wonderful World*, Grolier, New York, vol. 17; 'The Stone Age' in *The Encyclopedia Ameri-*

cana, International Edition, Americana Corporation, New York; 'Prehistoric Man' in *The World Book Encyclopedia*, Field Enterprises Educational Corporation, Chicago, Frankfurt, London, Sydney, Toronto, Vol. 15; 'Stone Age', *ibid.*, Vol. 18. Vol. 18.

4 Third edition, by John Cooke, Hodges Figgis, Dublin, 1903, p. 188.

5 'Despite much searching for palaeoliths, and occasional claims which have proved false . . . there is no evidence that Ireland was occupied either during any of the interglacial periods . . . or during the last phase of the glacial age': Estyn Evans, *Prehistoric and Early Christian Ireland*, Batsford, London, 1966, p. 6. 'There are no certain traces of a Palaeolithic (Old Stone Age) habitation in Ireland': Harry Perceval Swan, *Highlights of Ireland's Story*, Dundalgan Press, Dundalk, 1969, p. 2. See also Joseph Raftery 'Archaeology Introduction', *Encyclopedia of Ireland*, p. 65; G. F. Mitchell, 'Quaternary Era', *ibid.*, p. 39.

6 The remains of the Rosses Point shelter can be easily seen and visited from the beach. The Coney Island cave is on Carraig Mairtín on the south west shore.

7 I am indebted to Dr. Joseph Raftery, Director of the National Museum of Ireland, for assistance with written sources on the Sligo sites. Dr. Raftery's book *Prehistoric Ireland* (Batsford, London, 1951) is a standard work on this subject.

8 Reid Moir's published works include *The Antiquity of Man in East Anglia*, Cambridge University Press, 1927.

9 W. E. Harrison, Ipswich, Suffolk, 1928.

10 *Nature*, Vol. 120, 20 August 1927, p. 261.

11 pp. 9–11. The term 'quaternary' (from the Latin word for 'four') is used to describe the latest chapter in the earth's history. 'The Quaternary Era is the fourth of the major units into which geological time has been divided. It opens, perhaps two million years ago, with the first appearance of man, or man-like creatures. It is subdivided into the Pleistocene Period, or Great Ice Age . . . and the Holocene Period, the time since the last of the great ice masses shrank away, about 10,000 B.C.' 'Quaternary Era' by Professor G. F. Mitchell, in *Encyclopedia of Ireland*, p. 38.

12 pp. 12, 13.

13 It should be noted that during the ice-age, when the Mousterian culture existed in the lowlands which were free of ice, the sea level was low because much of the world's water was frozen on higher ground. Ireland and England were connected by land with the Continent. By about the year 6,000 B.C. enough ice had melted to cut off Ireland from England.

14 p. 19.

15 Cf. 'The Exploration of the Caves of Keshcorran, County Sligo', R. F. Scharff and Others, *Trans. Roy. Irish Acad.*, Vol. 33, Sect. B, pp. 171–214; Robert Lloyd Praeger, *The Way That I Went*, pp. 140, 141.

16 p. 114. Cf. O. T. Jones and P. G. H. Boxwell, 'Geological Features of the Sites of the Sligo Implements', *Nature*, Vol. 121, 2 June 1928, pp. 861, 862. Also, J. K. Charlesworth and R. A. S. Macalister, 'The Alleged Palaeolithic Instruments of Sligo', *Proc. Roy. Irish Acad.*, Vol. 39, Section 3, pp. 18–32.

17 Burchell and Reid Moir, p. 20.

18 *Ibid.*, p. 19. Cf. 'Palaeolithic Man in N.W. Ireland', Occasional Paper No. 1, *Prehist. Soc. East Anglia*, 1929, pp. 1–15.

19 *The Way That I Went*, pp. 140, 141; cf. also *ibid.*, p. 259 on the Giant Deer or 'Irish Elk' which, though not an exclusively Irish animal, was especially abundant in Ireland in Palaeolithic times.

20 *The Mountains of Ireland*, p. 53. Before leaving this fascinating subject, three points should be noted. The case for rapid marine erosion on the Coney Island site made by Jones and Boxwell, and accepted by Macalister, Charlesworth and Movius, appears to be based principally on 'the beacon (which) was erected near the edge of the cliff. The concrete base of the beacon has now been undermined by the collapse of the cliff over the cave. . . .' (Jones and Boxwell, *Nature*, Vol. 121, 1928, p. 862; cf. Charlesworth and Macalister, *Proc. R.I.A.*, Vol. 39, 1930, Section C, pp. 24, 25; Movius, *The Irish Stone Age*, pp. 108 ff.) When I discovered that the oldest inhabitants of Coney Island had never even heard of a beacon at this point, I consulted Mr. Michael Costello of the Commissioners of Irish Lights, Dublin, and Mr. John McMeekin, Sligo Harbour Master, who confirmed that between the present time

and 1860 there was never a beacon at this point on Coney Island and, before 1860, it was most unlikely that any sort of navigational light existed on the island. The only beacons on the island were erected at the northern end in 1908, and were removed in 1977. Being a navigational light, a beacon could not have been erected without the knowledge and, indeed, the authority of the Commissioners of Irish Lights or their predecessors, the Corporation for Preserving and Improving the Port of Dublin, and the Port of Dublin Corporation, to which various Acts of Parliament transferred all functions, powers and duties in relation to lighthouses and beacons around the coast of Ireland (cf. *A Short History of the Commissioners of Irish Lights*, Irish Lights Office, Dublin, 1976).

The second point worth noting is that Jones and Boxwell, who headed the 'geological attack' on Burchell, and who subsequently were regarded as the leading authorities on the geology of the Sligo sites, had not, when they wrote, examined or even seen any of the stone implements on which Burchell based his claims, even though the stones had been exhibited in London.

Thirdly, although Movius maintains that Burchell's finds must 'be rejected as conclusive evidence for a palaeolithic settlement in Ireland' (*The Irish Stone Age*, p. 111), he does agree that the Rosses Point and Coney Island implements examined by him 'seem to be definitely human artefacts' (*loc. cit.*); and, when dealing with the Ballyconnel implements, he concludes : 'If, on the other hand, further research should bring to light additional specimens of demonstrably human origin, then man must have been in Ireland during the last inter-glacial period prior to the deposit of the Boulder Clay' (*loc. cit.*). His general conclusion, however, is : 'If Ireland were occupied during the palaeolithic period, these sites cannot be accepted as proof of it, since the evidence is unsound and inconclusive' (p. 114).

This verdict in 1942 by the accepted authority on Stone Age Ireland was regarded as the end of the Sligo controversy which had begun in 1927. Recently, however, the conclusions of Movius himself in his book *The Irish Stone Age* have been questioned and, according to Liam de Paor, they 'now require fundamental modification' ('The New Archaeology', *The Irish Times*, 26 October 1976, p. 8).

All of which suggests that we may not yet have heard the end of the Sligo sites and Mousterian Man !

84

21 Cf. 'Ethiopia Yields First "Family" of Early Man', Donald C. Johanson, PH.D., *National Geographic*, Vol. 150, No. 6, December 1976, pp. 791–811; *Prehistoric and Primitive Man*, Andreas Lommel, pp. 14 ff.

22 Michael Herity and George Eogan, *Ireland in Prehistory*, Routledge and Kegan Paul, London, Henley and Boston, 1977, p. 16. This is the first major synthesis on Irish archaeology since Joseph Raftery's *Prehistoric Ireland* appeared in 1951. The authors accept the view of Charlesworth and Macalister on the Sligo sites (*loc. cit.*). In their preface, however, they indicate that neither of them specialises in the Palaeolithic Age and that 'both writers are well aware that alternative selections of material and other interpretations can be put forward, particularly in the areas in which they are not specialists' (p. xiii).

17 Fairies and Faeryland

1 'Kidnappers', *Mythologies*, p. 70. The spellings 'Fairyland' and 'Faeryland' are both used; Yeats preferred 'Faeryland'.

2 *History of Sligo* (1691–1891) p. 314. The more correct spelling for Pollnamaddow is Pollnamada (Irish for 'the dogs' hole'). The spelling used in marine charts is Pollnamadoo.

3 *Wakeman's Handbook of Irish Antiquities*, Hodges, Figgis, Dublin, 1903, p. 160. Wakeman's estimate was probably based on the six-inch sheets of the Irish Ordnance Survey which mark over 30,000 ring forts. See *Ireland in Prehistory*, Michael Herity and George Eogan, pp. 225–228; see 'Problems of Irish Ring Forts', Michael J. O'Kelly, *The Irish Sea Province in Archaeology and History*, edited by Donald Moore, Cambrian Archaeological Association, Cardiff, 1970, p. 50.

4 *A History of Irish Fairies*, Carolyn White, The Mercier Press, Dublin and Cork, 1976, p. 7.

5 *Sligo and Its Surroundings*, pp. 209–211.

6 *The Yeats Country*, p. 41.

7 *Sligo and Its Surroundings*, pp. 210, 211. John McGowan's comment reminds me of the comment made by Peats Sheamuis of the Great Blasket Island (three miles west of County Kerry) to Robin Flower : 'Maybe there are fairies and maybe not, but

everybody knows there are things outside of this world, and they do things that no power in this world could do. And I know that for myself, for I have seen it with my own eyes' (*The Western Island or The Great Blasket*, Robin Flower, Clarendon Press, Oxford, 1971, p. 134).

8 The duties involved were defined as 'lighting, extinguishing and attending' the lights in Sligo River. See *The Sligo Star*, 26 July 1900; *The Sligo Independent*, 25 July 1901; *The Sligo Champion*, 25 July 1901.

9 On a prominence at the eastern extremity of Coney Island, behind Michael James Ward's public house, there are the remains of a star-shaped fort which, according to some local antiquarians, dates from Cromwellian times. Coney Island featured in Cromwell's proposals for planting the Sligo region.

What appear to be the remains of another earthen ring can be seen at the northern end of the island, overlooking the area known as Sean Bhaile (Irish for 'the old townland') which is on the right-hand side of the road to Carty's Strand. It should be noted that not all 'ring forts' are in fact rings. For this reason Michael J. O'Kelly writes : 'There is something to be said in favour of using the word *rath* as a general term instead of ring fort and this may yet be done' (*op. cit.*, pp. 50, 51). 'There seems to be hardly a barony in County Sligo that is not linked with faery legend or religion or ancient battle' (Lennox Robinson in 'Bryan Cooper').

10 This is from a longer extract of a Milne poem on Sligo given in *Sligo and Its Surroundings*, Tadhg Kilgannon, p. 211. Another poem of Milne is quoted by Kilgannon *op. cit.*, p. 206. For a biographical note on Milne see note 2 of the following chapter.

18   Knocknarea

1 'Red Hanrahan's Song about Ireland'.

2 Another Sligo poet, R. J. Milne, has also written about Knocknarea, in the shadow of which he was born and reared :

> Hill of Kings and mystic mountain,
> Theme of song and legends old —
> As I watch the purple shadows
> In the sunset change to gold,
> How I dream of all thy greatness.

86

Robert J. Milne (1873–1918) was born at Knocknarea, Co. Sligo, and died in Manchester, Massachusetts, U.S.A. He published poems (many of them about Sligo) in Irish and American newspapers and journals. Members of the Milne family still reside at Knocknarea. The poet's daughter, Mrs. Kathleen Raftery (to whom I am indebted for information about her father), resides in Sligo.

3 For information on this place name, and on many others in the Sligo region, consult James P. McGarry, *Place Names in the Writings of William Butler Yeats*, Colin Smythe, Gerrards Cross, 1976, p. 62 *et passim*. See also John O'Donovan, *Name Books of Sligo*, No. 118, and Kilgannon's *Almanac and Business Directory for North Connacht*, Sligo, 1906, p. 138.

4 Some say that it is King Eoghan Bell who is buried under the cairn. This theory fits the name 'Hill of the Kings' better, but it aggravates the problem of chronology for Eoghan Bell, as we shall see, died in 537 A.D. Praeger (*The Way That I Went*, p. 142) suggests that 'the huge Knocknarea cairn may have been a cenotaph' for Queen Maeve. Writing on the Knocknarea Cairn, Stephen Rynne comments : 'since the scholars have taken history out of the hands of the simple traditionalists one knows nothing for certain' (*All Ireland*, Batsford, London, 1956, p. 172). For a delightful summary of the exploits of Queen Maeve, see *The Pegasus Book of Ireland*, Helen O'Clery, Dennis Dobson, London, 1967, pp. 129–132. For a vivid account of the fortunes of Eoghan Bell's two sons, one of whom (Ceallach) became a bishop and was murdered, see *Stories from O'Dowda's Country*, Gertrude O'Reilly, pp. 39–44.

5 According to Praeger (*op. cit.*, p. 143) at least two hundred sepulchral monuments existed 'until comparatively lately'.

6 The reader should see the concise but informative brochure, entitled *Pre-historic Sligo*, published by the North-Western Regional Tourism Organisation.

19   Oisín in Tír na nOg

1 Glenasmole is a valley about seven miles south of Dublin — the river Dodder flows through the valley.

2 I made the above summary of the story of Oisín from P. W. Joyce's translation in *Old Celtic Romances*, pp. 259–268. A

good account in Gaelic of this Ossianic tale will be found in *An Fhiannuidheacht*, Cormac O Cadhlaidh, Foillseacháin Rialtais, Baile Atha Cliath, 1937, pp. 321 ff. The interested reader should consult two small books by the late Gerard Murphy who was Professor of the History of Celtic Literature at University College, Dublin. They are *The Ossianic Lore and Romantic Tales of Medieval Ireland*, and *Saga and Myth in Ancient Ireland*, both published by the Mercier Press, Cork, for the Cultural Relations Committee of Ireland. 'The story of Oisín is in Leonie's Irish book,' said my niece Olivia (who read this book page by page as it was typed). She was referring to her sister's Primary School Third Class Gaelic Reader, *Sraith Na Cainte*, Leabhar F, 1976, pp. 30 ff. For young readers an excellent introduction to the heroes of ancient Ireland is the shortened edition of Standish O'Grady's *Fionn and His Companions* (illustrated by Bríd Ní Rinn), The Talbot Press, Dublin, 1970.

20 Dunán Pádraig

1 *History of Sligo* (1691–1891), p. 363.

2 The word Mulclohy is derived from the Irish word for 'stone'. The present-day English form of Mulclohy is Stone or Stoney.

3 *History of Sligo*, I, p. 359. The historian W. G. Wood-Martin, an authority on Sligo fisheries, refers to the surprising fact 'that the Sligo and Ballysadare rivers, being in such close proximity, should differ so much in the dates of their respective fishing seasons, the principal run of fish in the former being in January, in the latter in May.' (*History of Sligo*, 1691–1891, p. 257). Another historian, McTernan, says that 'naturalists have been unable to account for this strange phenomenon' (*Historic Sligo*, p. 49). Kilgannon also comments : 'It certainly is inexplicable the difference between the salmon of Sligo and Ballisodare rivers' (*Sligo and Its Surroundings*, p. 112).

21 Cummen Strand and the Fourteen Pillars

1 Cummen is also spelled Cummeen, Cumen and Cummin.

2 The Ormsbys were prominent among the landed gentry of County Sligo from the mid-seventeenth to the nineteenth century (they held over 30,000 acres). The last of the Ormsbys

to reside at Cummen was Charles who was a Deputy Lieutenant for County Sligo from 1838 to 1849. The Sligo Ormsbys were related to the Ormsbys of Tobervaddy in Roscommon.

3 Report on Meeting of Sligo Harbour Commissioners, *The Sligo Champion*, 7 February, 1880.

4 For this information I am indebted to Sligo wildbird expert, Mr. Noel Murphy who was organiser of research on County Sligo for *The Atlas of Breeding Birds in Britain and Ireland* published in 1976. For an informative note on the Brent Goose see *A List of the Birds of Ireland*, Robert F. Ruttledge, pp. 30, 31.

5 Cf. 'St. Patrick's Coney Island', *Fortnightly Review*, March 1950, p. 194. The last occupants of 'Island House' were the Flood family. Jack Flood, with his wife (Delia Ward, sister of islanders Michael James Ward and Mrs. Tessie McGowan) and their three children emigrated to the United States in 1928.

6 The Grand Juries were forerunners of the present County Councils.

7 *History of Sligo* (1691–1891), p. 384.

8 In 1975 Sligo County Council repaired and pointed the pillars. Residents of the island are now hopeful that a new road above the level of sand and tide will soon be provided. They point out that during the last quarter of a century several people, especially visitors to the island and holidaymakers, have lost their way in fog and on dark nights. 'You need a road as well as pillars,' says islander John McGowan who will never forget the night when, as a boy, he helped the men of Coney Island to avert another tragedy on the strand in the early 1950's.

At 11.30 p.m. the County Hospital ambulance left the island with a man suffering from acute appendicitis. The driver of the ambulance lost his way and drove in the direction of the channel between Strandhill and Coney Island. Fortunately, Michael James Ward saw the ambulance going off course and immediately alerted the men of the island : Pakie Haran, Tommy Carty, Tommy McLoughlin, Dan McGowan, Roger McFadden and young John McGowan. When the men reached the ambulance it was already embedded in the soft, wet sand, the frightened occupants being unable to do anything. With spades, shovels and large stones the men managed, after three hours of strenuous work, to get the heavy vehicle up on planks from which it was pushed back on course. 'It was three o'clock in the morning when we got it dug out, and not a minute too soon. The incoming tide was just beginning to cover the strand.'

John McGowan still speaks with admiration of Nurse Begley who, during the ordeal, displayed great calmness and courage in comforting the seriously-ill patient (who was the late Luke Carty).

When driving a car to the island one should always keep to the left of the pillars until the thirteenth pillar (the second-last one from the island) is passed. Immediately this second last pillar is passed one should take a 45° right-hand turn and head straight for the two small concrete bollards marking the entrance to the island's road. These bollards or small pillars are a little to the right of the imposing abandoned 'Island House'.

9 Bryan MacMahon, *Here's Ireland*, Batsford, London, 1971, p. 174. For additional interesting glimpses of Sligo, see *Wonders of Ireland*, Eric Newby and Diana Petry, Hodder and Stoughton, London, 1969, pp. 167–178; *Illustrated Road Book of Ireland*, The Automobile Association, Dublin, 1970.

> We shall never meet a spot so sweet
> As the beautiful city of Sligo.
> — Alfred Percival Graves

Acknowledgments

In the Notes I have acknowledged my indebtedness to many who obliged me with information and advice. The following have also kindly helped: John McGowan and Mrs. Margaret McGowan, Desmond Rushe, Jim McGarry, John Keohane, Dr. Frank Egan, Mrs. Brega Murphy, Kevin Murray and Mrs. Peg Murray, B. F. Rhattigan, Captain C. C. Lestrange, Jack and Tom Kilfeather, Bernard McDonagh, Austie Gillen, Willie Bruen, Mary Lappin, Mrs. Teresa McCauley, Mrs. Maura Gilligan and Mrs. Margaret Finnegan.

I am also grateful to the eminent historian Cardinal Tomás Ó Fiaich, Archbishop of Armagh, who read the final typescript and corrected some inaccuracies, and to Senator Michael B. Yeats and other holders of copyright in the sources quoted. If any inadvertent infringement of copyright has occured, sincere apologies are offered, and the error will be rectified in future editions.

T.A.F.

The critics said of the first printing of SLIGO:

'. . . written with loving and scholarly attention to detail' (*The Sunday Press*); 'a treasure trove . . . almost compulsory reading for Yeatsian study' (*Western Journal*); '. . . fascinating . . . excellently brought out . . . full of interesting facts and lore' (*The Irish Independent*); 'So readable and so full of interest' (*Roscommon Herald*); 'This is another relaxed guide to have in your hand, as you set out in the footsteps of the Poet (Yeats), to explore the beauties and wonders of Sligo' (*Hibernia*); 'Good research . . . a book which can be read and re-read from cover to cover, or kept close by and dipped into in a quite moment' (*The Sligo Champion*).